F
Joh   Johnston, Norma

              Strangers dark
              and gold

DATE DUE

STRANGERS
DARK
AND GOLD

STRANGERS
DARK
AND GOLD

Norma Johnston

ATHENEUM   NEW YORK   1975

FOR ROBERT AND HELLA REEVES

"The companions of Wisdom, helpers of men
In every kind of excellence . . ."
"Judgement and right counsel are yours."
(Euripides; Pindar)

Map by Guy Fleming

LIBRARY OF CONGRESS CATALOGING IN PUBLICATION DATA
Johnston, Norma.   Strangers dark and gold.
SUMMARY: Recounts the Greek myth of Jason, his search
with the Argonauts for the Golden Fleece, and the final
tragedy resulting from Medea's love for him.
1. Jason—Juvenile literature. [1. Jason. 2. Mythology, Greek]
I. Title. PZ8.1.J64St 292'.2'13 74-19463
ISBN 0-689-30451-x

Published simultaneously in Canada by
McClelland & Stewart, Ltd.
Manufactured in the United States of America by
The Book Press, Brattleboro, Vermont
Designed by Suzanne Haldane
First Edition

CONTENTS

STRANGERS DARK AND GOLD

Isle of Amber

River Eridanius (Po R.)

TYRRHEN

Stoechades Is.

AUSONIAN SEA

Elba

Aea
Home of Cir

RHONE RIVER

M E D I T E R

Miles

0   100   200   300   400   500

Route of Jason and the Argonauts

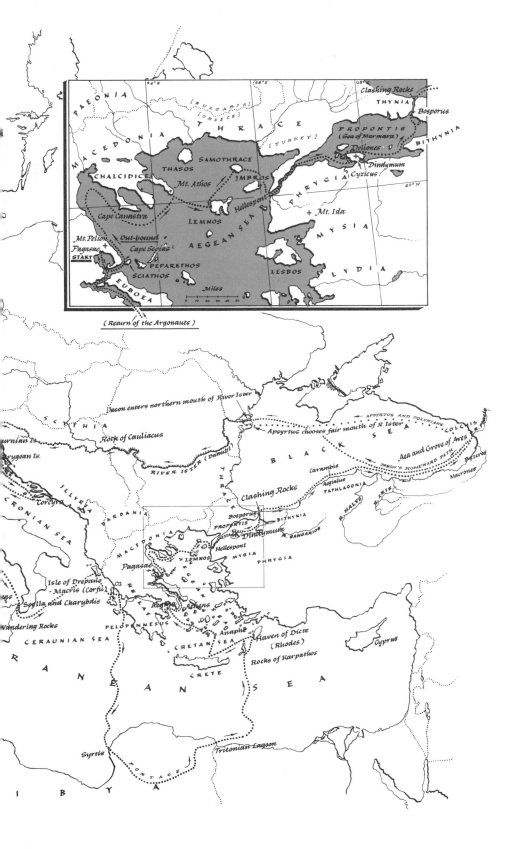

(Return of the Argonauts)

PROLOGUE

ENVY AND LUST began it. Envy and passion, rejection turned to hate, fear of a rival. And an aging man's lusting after his lost youth. It began, as it was to end, in tears and blood. And the gods, if they were looking on at us, must have laughed. Or wept.

Many things the gods achieve beyond our judgement.
What we thought is not confirmed,
And what we thought not,
God contrives.

I know.

You who are young, whose blood is hot and whose hearts and bodies throb with all you know and do not know, hear me. I sing of love and hate and too much giving, and of the Stranger —the stranger in a strange land; the stranger in us all.

Athamas, king of Orchomenus, was growing old. And he looked upon Ino, golden Ino, young daughter of Cadmus, king of Thebes, and lusted for her. Ino was yet a virgin and, the world thought, innocent, and Athamas desired her. The fact

3

that he already had a wife, the noble Nephele, deterred him not at all.

For Nephele was a great lady who long since, like her lord, had drunk the wine of youth. Now she was to taste the bitter dregs, the rejection by the husband she had honored, who had shared her bed and whose children she had borne. Had she been barren, the world, the gods and even she herself would have understood; a king must have an heir. But Athamas could make no such excuse. The youth, prince Phrixus, was his parents' pride. There was a sister, too, the little Helle. All this Athamas thrust from his mind, which was possessed with images of Ino.

Ino, the Golden One, granddaughter so men said of Aphrodite and the God of War. She had the face of that queen of love, but also Aphrodite's cunning, and a serpent heart. And when she was given in marriage by her father to the already matured and wedded Athamas, she did not protest.

Cadmus should have known better. He had ruled over Thebes with wealth and wisdom, and he was known through all the civilized world as a good king. Yet he gave his daughter Ino in marriage to the married Athamas.

When the news came to her, Nephele wept. She wept as a cast-off wife, but also as a mother, for she felt dark fears.

"Why should this golden girl look kindly on my son, on Athamas' first-born? Phrixus is heir to the kingdom, and Athamas adores him. And so at first Ino will pay lip-tribute. But later, when the honeymoon begins to wane, when her childishness begins to bore him and her body, swollen big with child, is no longer pleasing, she will begin to think. She will not want a son of the first marriage to inherit, she will protect the interests of her own children, and Phrixus' life will not be safe."

Nephele was right, for she knew how crafty a mind can be. But she had not guessed the darker shadow that sped Phrixus' doom. Even as Athamas had looked on Ino and desired her, so

Ino looked on Phrixus and grew sick with passion, preferring the stalwart half-grown youth to the aging bridegroom.

The young Phrixus, understanding at last, grew pale with loathing. He resented the wrong done to his mother and now this greater insult offered to his father, and he repelled the advances of the stepmother so close to him in age. And in Ino's breast love turned to hate, and she began to think, as Nephele had predicted, of the interests of her own future children. And her mind wrought a hellish pattern of revenge.

It was the custom each year in Orchomenus to hold at planting-time a festival of fertility in honor of the earth-mother, goddess of the harvest. All the seed corn saved from the previous harvest was taken before the altar and blessed. And throughout the land the men of each household, from the king to the lowest slave, went out into the fields on the longest day of the year, and with hymns of praise and sacrifices and wine-offerings, they sowed the seed in the new-made furrows; and when warm night fell, they lay down in the fresh fields, each man with his own woman, and they blessed the fertile life-giving seeds with their own bodies. And the young Ino also went out with her husband the king, who greatly loved her. But as she lay looking up at the silver moon above his greying head, her heart was filled with an unholy triumph, for she knew the blessing she had wrought for the hungry fields was barren.

All the corn for the country, for all men's fields, had been brought before the altar to be consecrated, and from there, the next day, had been divided, so much to each. But in the time between, unseen, Ino had stolen before the altar, taken the seed, and parched it over fire until all the life in every kernel was dry and dead. And all that long summer, no wheat waved like a golden sea across the arid fields of all the land. The days grew hot, the sun scorched the people's anxious faces, the bees hummed restlessly, and there was no harvest. For the bitter winter yet to come, there would be no bread.

The people's hearts were filled with strange foreboding. If the gods behaved so cruelly, it could only be because of some great wrong. They turned to their king and leader, whose heart was sorrowing for his starving people. Ino put a mask of sympathy across the face of triumph and pleaded with her husband.

"It is right they turn to you, for you are the greatest and wisest in the country. A king is father to his subjects and must take care of them. But you, who are highest of all men in the land, do not know the answer. To whom can you yourself turn to, save the gods?"

"You are right," Athamas said, and because his heart was filled with pity for his people, he sent a messenger to the Delphic oracle.

"What wrong has brought this curse upon our people?" Athamas bid him ask. "What sacrifice and amends must we make to right the wrong?"

The secret of what happened next is locked in the dark recesses of the woman's heart. Some say the messenger, sick himself with love for Ino, allowed himself to be corrupted; some say the wily queen seduced the very Delphic priest himself.

Back to King Athamas came the message: "A curse is on your country. Until the young Prince Phrixus is sacrificed upon the altar, no corn will grow."

When he heard these words, Athamas grew pale and his recaptured youth fled from him, never to return. And through all the starving land the wailing grew. In the night Queen Ino wooed her heavyhearted husband with wily words.

"Father you are to Phrixus, but also to your people. A king's burden is greater than ordinary men's, for he must think of the greatest good for all." She took his hand and placed it over her quickening womb, murmuring, "There will be other sons."

In the still heat of the morning, Athamas sat like stone. He knew the torment of Prometheus, who also had tried to do good for mortal men and had had the cost torn from his very vitals. Athamas could feel the eagle's talons tearing at his guts at the thought of sacrificing his beloved son. But Ino was right. A king's first responsibility was to his people. He must not put private loyalties ahead of public good.

He bowed and turned the prince, Phrixus, over to the priests for sacrifice. The people rejoiced, and Ino masked her triumph, and Phrixus' sister, the child Helle, stood beside the altar weeping. Unseen by the crowd, the Furies, who avenge all crimes of blood, looked on with implacable eyes.

The priest raised his knife. Nephele's heart, almost bursting within her, sent out a last piteous prayer, and the gods relented. Down from the skies on a shaft of sunlight that blinded the watcher's eyes, came a great golden Ram. When men could look again, the altar was empty of Phrixus and his sister Helle. They had flown off through the air, clinging to the great Ram's golden fleece.

The Ram flew far to the north-northeast, and as they passed over the strait that separates Europe from Asia, legend tells, Helle leaned too far outward, looking down, and lost her grip on the Ram's fleece. She fell off and was drowned in the waters far below. That is why, men say, the strait in which she drowned is still called the Hellespont, or Helle's Bridge. Phrixus saw it happening and reached out, but dared not reach too far lest he lose his own grip, and so could not save her.

Still the Ram soared on, over the Caucasian peak where Prometheus was chained, over wild barbarous country, and at last came safely to land in the country of Colchis, on the Unfriendly Sea. There Phrixus sacrificed the Ram that had saved him to Zeus, the God of Flight. He said afterwards the Ram itself had bid him do it. Man always does prefer to be rid of those to whom much gratitude is owed.

The Colchians were a fierce people who did not welcome strangers, and their king, Aetes, descendant of the Sun, was the most austere and wiliest of all. He did not know what to make of this golden youth who seemed to have come on the rays of the setting sun. A stranger, yes, Aetes thought, but obviously divinely blessed. He thought so even more when Phrixus, who was not a fool, offered him the Golden Fleece as a sacred treasure. So in return Aetes gave Phrixus his own daughter, Chalciope, as wife.

I have been told Chalciope wept and moaned to Hecate, preferring death, when she was told that she must surrender herself to the alien stranger.

In the kingdom of Orchomenus, the altar was empty. The people were appalled, thinking the gods were mocked. They turned upon their king, Athamas, and would have sacrificed him in substitution, except that some men spoke of having seen the golden Ram flying off with Phrixus on the shaft of light.

"Wait," they counseled. "Surely this could only have been done by the gods. We must wait and see what the gods and the Fates may bring."

So the people waited, and the next year the crops grew, and in time travelers brought back news that Phrixus was safe in Colchis. Some few years later came the news of his death. That was all! Colchis was a far and unfriendly land, and few travelers dared it and fewer yet returned.

In Orchomenus Athamas lived on and grew old, saw his wife Ino bear him two more sons, Learchus and Melicertes. And he, who had rejected his wife and partner in greatness for youth and lust, who had thought he must sacrifice his loved son to the gods to save his people, paid for his folly in a still more terrible way. He went mad and mistook his son Learchus for a wild beast, shooting him dead with his own hand. Next he turned on the child, Melicertes. The terrified Ino grabbed him up and ran, the child clinging to her neck, to the edge of the high cliffs. There she threw herself and the young son down into the sea, preferring this death to a more terrible one at her husband's hands. So the children perished, their blood shed as a result of their parents' selfish deeds. So the sorrowing Nephele was avenged. And the Furies smiled.

The Greeks say our futures are woven by three Fates who, knowing our natures, weave a pattern we could predict were we wise enough to know ourselves. Often, man being what he is, the pattern will repeat. Especially in families. So it would do now.

Athamas had a brother, Salmoneus, whose daughter Tyro was wife to Cretheus, king of Iolcus in Thessaly. She bore him three sons, Aeson, heir to the kingdom, and Pheras and Amythaon. But she had also borne two other sons, twin boys, whom she had abandoned, fearing her father's wrath for at the time she had no husband. Years later, when Cretheus learned of it, she claimed she had been made pregnant by Poseidon the ocean god. Cretheus did not believe it—or, if he did believe, would not forgive. He cast Tyro out and, heaping on grief, married her maid.

The twin boys had been found and reared by Salmoneus' keeper of the horses. Most appropriate, for horses were sacred to Poseidon and their long manes could often be seen in the sea waves. The infants, Pelias and Neleus, were reared in ignorance of their true parentage until Cretheus' death. Then their foster mother revealed to them the truth, and they went at once in search of their real mother. They found Tyro living in misery and squalor, persecuted by the second wife, Sidero. Pelias, in his anger, slew Sidero where she had taken refuge in Hera's temple. Thus he brought down upon himself, in time, the goddess' wrath.

Pelias was deprived of killing Cretheus by the fact that the old king was already dead. He did what seemed to him the next best thing. Biding his time, he at last succeeded in seizing the throne of Iolcus, deposing the king, his half-brother Aeson, who was Cretheus' rightful heir. He said he did it to avenge the wrong done by Cretheus to his mother, Tyro.

Pelias seized the throne and wealth, the scepter of absolute rule and the fields and sheep and tawny herds of oxen. He threw his half-brother and his queen Alcimede into squalor and darkness, but he dared not kill them, fearing the people's wrath. For all men know we bring the Furies of Hell upon our hearts when we kill our own blood kin. Nonetheless, he sought in secret for Aeson's death.

Alcimede was with child when this occurred, and the shock brought her to childbed. All night she labored, and when she heard her son's first cry, she feared for her infant's life. So when the dawning sun first opened the baby's eyes, she called her husband to her, and the women who had stayed faithful attendants in poverty. They darkened the house and drowned the infant's first wails in the sound of keening, gave out the news that a child had been born and died. As darkness fell, amid the wailing of women, the child was sent away by stealth, wrapped in purple swaddling clothes. Only night knew the secret of the road that was taken.

The boy was reared by Chiron the Centaur, half-man, half-horse, the gentle scholar who was son of the Titan Cronus. And the infant's name was Jason.

THE
YOUNG
STRANGER

I

ONE CAME
TO IOLCUS

I T WAS in the spring of his twentieth year that an idea in Jason's heart hardened into determination. Tall, young, and strong, he came swinging up through the white dust of the road that led towards Iolcus, his heart afire with righteous vengeance. His golden hair, which he had never cut, flamed down his sunburned back, and on his muscular legs he wore the close saffron trousers common in the Magnesian land. Across his bare shoulders he had flung a leopard skin to keep off the shivering rains. Jason—burning with zeal, out to right the wrongs done to his unknown father.

Behind him lay the quiet years, the years of obscurity in the cave-home in Mt. Pelion, taught by Chiron, that wise and gentle scholar. They had been years of loneliness and doubts, knowing he was not like other boys, yet not knowing why. Then, the age of understanding followed on the heels of a child's age of questions. They became years of learning bit by bit the truth of his ancestry, the tales of the great Prometheus, and of the Golden Fleece, and of far more interest to Jason, of Pelias the usurper and how he had stolen the throne by force.

13

Piece by piece through his youth he had learned the story, and the wise Chiron had counseled wisdom, counseled moderation, until at last the invisible bonds had snapped and Jason, feeling himself a man, would hear no more.

"I am going to right the wrong done to my father, Aeson. How else can I dare call myself a descendant of Aeolus!"

"Remember then," Chiron counseled wryly, "what it is you seek to do. To right an indignity done to one's blood kin is a cause the gods approve. But Pelias too is your blood kin. To shed that blood for your own advancement is another thing entirely."

Jason shook his head impatiently. "I know that! It's my father's honor that interests me. No more!"

But Chiron, watching his loved foster child set off through the pale dawn, had his own misgivings. He understood, too well, Jason's need for recognition and secure position.

Spring was on Thessaly, and everywhere on the hillsides the flowers were putting forth their reddest blossoms. The olive trees, gnarled with the weight of years, were leafing. The rivers were freshening, overflowing their banks from the spring rains. Jason swung along, his firm tread causing the wet leather of his sandals to squeak beneath his step. He had made those sandals himself, tanning the leather carefully, threading the leather thongs, for he wished to appear worthy of his rank when he stood before Pelias. He had not reckoned on the overflowing streams, which at intervals had turned the lowland paths into seas of mud.

"You ought to have carried the sandals. And the saffron trousers. Kept them safe for when there was good need to use them. A traveler need not look like a king's son," Chiron would have pointed out. Chiron had an annoying way of making Jason's lack of foresight explicitly clear.

The voice was so real in his thoughts that Jason's face darkened and his chin set. "Pride!" Chiron's imaginary voice chided. "Oh, Jason, Jason! When will you learn that that is the unforgivable sin, the sin against the gods? And in time it lays low all who indulge in it."

Involuntarily, Jason's hands formed fists, and he half stumbled on a rock in his path. Then, as he righted himself, the wet sandals gave forth a plaintive squish, and despite himself his brow cleared. Laughter bubbled up from deep within him.

"To land flat in the mud because I didn't look where I was going *would* be being brought low by pride! Don't think about it. Think about Pelias, who has monstrous pride and who is about to be brought low, but not by the gods. By Jason!"

As the sun rose hot in the sky, so did Jason's spirits, and he gloried in the scenes his mind created. Himself striding into the acropolis, or marketplace, of Iolcus, confronting Pelias of the pale heart. Pelias must be old by now. He would quake with fear at the wrath of Jason.

"But I will not take advantage," Jason thought, grinning. "It will be as I promised Chiron. No shedding of blood. No claiming of lands and wealth. Only the throne and scepter and my father's honor." He was young and the world lay before him. Lands, wealth and flocks he would gain in his own right in course of time.

Jason had chosen shrewdly the time for his dramatic entrance into Iolcus. It was Pelias' custom in the spring to hold a great festival to Poseidon. Poseidon the horse god; Poseidon, god of the seas; Poseidon, the father of Pelias, according to the legend that Pelias himself went to some pains to encourage. It not only invested him with divine lineage, but justified his seizing of the throne.

"My ancestry," Jason thought proudly, "is as good. And much more certain! From Prometheus, the benevolent Titan who gave fire to man." ("Prometheus means 'foresight,'" Chiron had said wryly. "Pray that your ancestor in time gives some to you.") "From Aeolus, the King of the Winds. And from Aeson, the rightful king of Iolcus."

This was another thing he would find in Iolcus, an answer he

wished and did not wish to know: what had become of Aeson?
For with it went the other question, never voiced, that had
stirred beneath the quiet surface of Jason's boyhood. If Aeson
or his consort Alcimede lived, why had they never sought to
claim their son? Years earlier he had pestered Chiron for
knowledge of his parents' fate. But Chiron, if he knew, had
never answered.

Ahead of Jason now lay the answer. He would find it where
he would find Pelias, in Iolcus at the festival.

Throughout all Thessaly the festival was famous, for prudent
Pelias had made it both religious ritual and holiday. He honored not only Poseidon, but the other gods as well, all except
Hera. To that jealous lady, sister-wife of Zeus, Pelias boasted
that he paid no homage.

"It might," Jason thought, "be worth my while to offer
prayers to Hera for assistance in my undertaking." Women,
even the goddesses, could be like hornets against those who
slighted them, and men were fools if they didn't take advantage
of that fact.

Certainly Pelias, the crafty, took advantage of the people's
religious superstitions to reinforce his own position with the
people. He gave them food, and wine, and a day free of labor.
He gave them a chance to wallow in superstition and feel vir-
tuous. He showed himself kind, and honorable, and respectful
of the Olympic gods, and descended from them. Not for a moment did Jason believe Pelias' piety to be sincere, for his own
would not have been, and he measured others by himself.

"Oh, he is clever, that one," Jason thought. "And I will learn
from him. It would be wise for me to continue this festival
when I am king."

When he was king! Jason's heart swelled fair to bursting
within him, and he threw back his head and gave vent to his
triumphant laughter. A few sheep, grazing on the rocky slopes,
gazed at him without curiosity. Otherwise there was none to
see or share. Jason didn't care. He liked the image he saw in

his mind's eye of himself the lone avenger, invincible in the justice of his cause, striding in where older and more experienced men had dared not step. It was a splendid picture.

After a minute he had to grin sheepishly at his own grandiloquence. "I will for certain fall on the rocks, if not in the mud, if I walk with my head up in the Olympian clouds and my eyes not on the road!" Chiron had taught him better, had taught him to pace himself at a manly stride, his eyes scanning both sky and road and roadside as he swung along, his two spears at the ready. The mountain roads of Thessaly presented human, as well as natural, dangers, and the wise centaur's own gentleness did not blind him to the evil ways of others.

But on this glorious day no dangers lurked. The sun was rising high in the sky and not even rain clouds threatened. The leopard skin was growing burdensome. "Let it stay!" Jason thought. Easier to wear than carry, and in the heat it proved its wearer was not afraid of some discomfort. Secretly Jason knew the pelt added dramatically to his appearance, but that was a consideration he would not acknowledge, even to himself. It was a garment such as kings would wear and only brave men won, and he, Jason, who had killed the beast himself, was the son of a king!

Ahead now lay the flooded river Anaurus and only a few more miles' easy travel. At the river's bank Jason permitted himself the luxury of rest, consuming the last of the wine and fruit that made up his provisions and then stretching out blissfully on his back beneath an arching tree to gaze at the blue sky and think great thoughts. He prolonged the interval to the last allowable moment, then jumped up to strip off the saffron trousers and make them and the wineskin into a bundle tied in the leopard's pelt upon his shoulders. Like an athlete, wearing only sandals, he waded into the river, and the cool water felt bracing to his skin. He could swim across easily, still keeping the bundle dry, so he stood for a moment, eyes measuring the distance, glorying in his power.

It was in that moment the unwelcome voice reached him.

"Young sir!" The voice came from an old crone hobbling along the riverbank. Where had she come from, Jason wondered in annoyance. And what in the name of Poseidon did she want? His time was short. But the voice was respectful, flattering in its very importuning. Jason lingered.

"Young master, surely you must be a god or son of a god. I am but an old woman, and helpless, but I must cross the river to pay honor to our father Poseidon. I beg you, carry me across on your shoulders that I may not miss the festival, and the gods will bless you."

Jason cursed beneath his breath. His own fault for lingering so long in pleasant fancies, otherwise he would have been long since across the river and on his way. This would delay him more, for he would have to ford the stream on foot and carefully. Then other thoughts came hard upon him. "The gods will bless you." Surely the old hag would pray for him out of gratitude. More, she would talk, old women always did, and the story of his magnanimity would spread among the common people at the festival. When he took the throne from Pelias, this would serve him well.

He turned, gave the old woman his most gracious smile, and knelt to permit her to mount on his shoulders. Her weight was surprisingly heavy for one so seeming frail, but he stood determinedly erect as he waded once again into the streaming waters.

With her muttered blessings and her gift of a few figs, he gave her courteous dismissal on the other shore after setting her on her tottering feet. It was then, straightening, that he became aware of his own feet. Foot, rather. One of his sandals was missing, lost in the mud of the river's bottom. Why had he not listened to the prudent voice in his own head and taken them off, regardless of possible hidden rocks!

He could not go back to search, for he must make up for the time already lost. Otherwise he would arrive as day was waning and the crowds had thinned. Not at all as he so long had planned, with the main square crowded with spectators and the sun gilding his bronzed body and bright hair! One sandal off, one on, he set off at a brisk run on the path to Iolcus.

On the outskirts of the city he stopped long enough to unroll his bundle, don the saffron trousers and fling the leopard skin again around his shoulders. Then, holding his two spears, he strode fearlessly into the throngs of the main square. And the people, in awe and wonder, gave way to let him pass.

Jason looked neither left nor right, as became a young lord, but his keen ear caught the murmurs as he passed. "A terrible man!" "Is it Apollo?" "No, nor Aphrodite's bronze-charioted lord." "Is it Otos, the giant, or his brother, daring Ephialtas, sons of Poseidon?" "They died, it is said, at bright Naxos." "Nor can it be Tityos, bright son of Earth, slain by Artemis' swift arrow." "It is a stranger . . . a stranger . . . a bright stranger. . . ."

Gradually the words changed. "*The* stranger . . . *the golden stranger . . . the young lord. . . .*" And everywhere, over and over, the same words: "The prophecy . . . *the prophecy is fulfilled!*"

What prophecy? Jason wondered shrewdly. Obviously, he had arrived at some fortunate time. But he must not betray himself by careless questioning. Rather assume himself the young lord expected, and in short time, by careful inquiries, learn who it was that was expected and how it might be to his advantage.

Across the square a cloud of dust signaled a chariot's approach, and silence swept through the crowd. In something Jason correctly judged as fear, the people parted. A burnished car drawn by mules jerked to a stop in the center of the square. The reins, so sharply pulled, were held in the sinewy grip of a man in his late middle years but still haughty in bearing. Flint-like eyes swept Jason contemptuously up and down.

"From what kind of country do you claim to come, you

stranger? What gutter slut got you in her ancient womb? Tell me your race, and with no filthy lies."

Jason was rightly proud of how quickly he was able to fight down the hot anger the words caused in his heart. He answered gently but without fear, as Chiron had taught him.

"All men shall recognize the master I name. I come from the Pelion cave of the god-like Beast. I have seen twenty summers, and in all of them have said or done nothing that can bring me shame. Now I have come home, to claim the ancient honor of my father, once given by Zeus to the sons of Aiolos. This is my story. Good citizens, tell me—where is the house of my fathers who rode the white horses? I ask as a man of this land, come to no strange country."

A stillness lay over the square, a stillness extending to the haughty charioteer, who stood, reins held tautly. The challenge came from him in terse quiet. "Your name?"

Jason flung his head back proudly. "Jason, son of Aeson the King!"

THE
CHALLENGE

FTERWARDS JASON wished that he had been less intent on his own pride, that he had watched the reactions of the other man more closely. Things happened so quickly, he told himself in justification.

"Jason . . . Jason . . . Jason. . . ." The murmur traveled quickly through the crowds, and presently merged in magic with another. "*Aeson . . . Aeson . . .*" The crowd closed in—old people, trying to tell him that they knew his father; simple people, eager and awed to touch his leopard skin, his hair. Jason's heart swelled. He scarcely noticed as the charioteer turned abruptly, struck out with his whip to clear a narrow path, and whirled off in a cloud of dust.

"Aeson . . . Aeson . . . Aeson's house. . . ." Arms reached out to lift him on shoulders, bear him off down narrow streets. To Jason, accustomed to the open freshness of the countryside, the closeness seemed oppressive. Pelias, he thought, doubtless lived in better fashion. He had already judged shrewdly that this was a shabby part of town. To what mean fate had Aeson sunk in the last years of his life, Jason wondered, and his heart flamed with new anger against Pelias.

The crowd stopped. His bearers set him down before a narrow hovel with doorway so low he would have to stoop to enter. "Jason . . . *Jason* . . ." The chant had begun again. The skin that served as door was pushed aside and a man early old, and bent with suffering, emerged. He straightened, squinting in the sun's bright rays, and a sound, half gasp, half cry, broke from him.

It had never occurred to Jason that his father was still alive.

In that first moment his only reaction was numbness, through which came one thought. "Then it is Aeson who still is rightful king."

The crowd was pushing him forward, so that he had to bow his head to enter the low dwelling. Jason did so, feeling ill at ease and therefore angry. Why had he not considered the possibility and prepared accordingly? Why had Chiron not warned him? How, without looking like an awkward youth, did one properly greet a long-lost parent? No, parents. This aging, dumpy woman running forward to embrace him was his mother, Alcimede, once loveliest of women, of whom the child Jason had dreamed so often!

Aeson with courteous words was thanking the crowd, dismissing them in a way that left them well content, lowering the curtain of skin across the door. Then he turned, and Jason to his embarrassment saw that tears welled in his father's eyes. It was an awkward moment, and Jason detested awkwardness when it touched himself. To his infinite relief the silence was broken by voices in the street.

"Uncle!" The skin was flung aside, and two young men burst in, filling the small house with their own vitality. To Jason their presence brought relief, and he sensed it did for Aeson also.

"Jason, your cousins. Admatus, son of my brother Pheras. And Melampos, son of Amythaon." They were close to Jason in age, frank faced, and built like athletes—the sort of men with whom he could feel at home.

"Father is coming," Admatus announced, folding himself up on a floor cushion and contriving to dwarf the little room. "Amythaon, too. We sent runners for them as we heard the news. That's why we weren't among the panting herd in the public square."

Melampos grinned wryly. "That, and because Pelias was there. Public reunions are bad enough without their taking place under our loving uncle's eye."

Jason straightened. "Pelias! Was that he, in the bronze chariot?"

"Indeed it was. Drawn, most appropriately, by mules. Our uncle is not one of the proud horsemen, Jason."

"Oh, so forget Pelias! We don't need him to spoil this moment. This is a time for celebration. And for wine, and not a drop in the house!" Alcimede, Jason was amused to notice, was as flustered as any common housewife. This was a situation with which, fortunately, he could cope, and at the same time redeem his earlier awkwardness. He reached in the leather pouch hung from a thong around his neck and turned to the nearest cousin. "Admatus, take these coins—find a wineshop somewhere, will you? Get figs, too, grapes, anything you see."

"Trust me." Admatus nodded and slipped out unobtrusively.

Presently Pheras arrived, from his home near the Hypereian fountain, and then Amythaon, from Messana. With their coming, and with the wine soon after flowing freely, the awkward tension vanished. The men settled in a tight circle around the hearth-fire, for the spring night was chill, and Alcimede hovered happily, pressing fruit and honey cakes upon them. They were, all of them, Jason decided through a pleasant glow, men whom any man would be proud to claim as kin. But even as the Dionysian fog settled comfortably on their senses, one thought persisted.

If Aeson lived, if his brothers and their strong sons lived so close, why in twenty years had none lifted a hand to right the wrong done him by their kinsman, Pelias?

For five nights without ceasing, Jason played host to his kinsmen in his father's house. For five days they spent the great luxurious hours in appropriate feasting, and Jason entertained them pleasantly with words honey-sweet. He watched, biding his time, remembering Chiron's constant counsel of patience. And on the sixth morning, at last, his hour came.

Melampos, who had slipped out to buy more wine, came back looking wary. "The guards are out. Casually wandering the street. Pelias is on the alert."

"Against what?" Jason demanded.

"Against you, cousin," Melampos retorted grinning. "You and the prophecy."

"Prophecy?" Jason asked innocently. But his ears pricked. This was the moment for which he had been waiting, keeping his own head clear of wine these past six days.

Melampos and Admatus exchanged glances, but it was the older Amythaon who answered. "Some time since, Pelias consulted the Oracle at Delphi, navel-stone of earth. He was told it had been appointed he should die 'by the hands of Aiolos' proud sons or their unrelenting counsels.' And he was told to beware at all costs a man who came wearing one sandal."

"As you did, Jason," Admatus said pointedly.

Jason answered carefully, choosing his words. "It is true I came to Iolcus seeking the overthrow of Pelias the usurper. Perhaps the gods even were responsible for my sandal's loss. I have heard tales of Hera disguising herself as an old woman to work her will. But tell me this, cousins and uncles. These twenty years you have lived nearer than I to Iolcus. You have known my father Aeson, known his suffering, when I did not. Yet you have tolerated Pelias without lifting up a hand against him. Tell me why."

"Pelias also is our kinsman, and he is crafty, and has power. Moreover, there are those who think Pelias deserves the throne because of the wrong done our mother Tyro by our father Cretheus. You are young, Jason. As one grows older, one learns to come to terms with fate." Pheras smiled, which infuriated Jason.

"Are you sure compromise is not another name for fear?"

Admatus' fists doubled and he started forward, but his father Pheras' swift hand detained him.

"Wait." Pheras' voice was quiet. "Jason has something to say to us, I think. Listen, and you may wish to take action with him, rather than against him."

"I thank you, uncle." Jason drew a deep breath and felt his heart beat and his voice grow steady. Chiron had taught him this, and he knew its value and followed the teaching when he could remember. In the moment's pause, he was able to organize his thoughts and he spoke with sober words, painting a picture of his lonely childhood, his wise counselor, his long dream of setting right Pelias' heinous wrong. "And so I have come," he finished, "to confront the usurper; I will not call him uncle. I mean to avenge the insult to the sons of Aeolus, and to claim the throne—for my father Aeson."

Aeson, lying wrapped on the couch where exhaustion had driven him, shook his head. "Not for me, Jason. I am now no fit king. Claim it for yourself if you will; you are my heir. But hear me now. Pelias is my brother by our mother Tyro. For her sake, lift no hand in anger. Demand the throne and title, if you will, for the gods are pleased when injustice is corrected. But touch not Pelias' fields, his sheep and oxen. The people will think better of you for it, and I have noticed men yield position quicker if their wealth is not likewise threatened."

"It was my very thought," Jason responded quickly. He jumped up from his couch and stood facing them, the sunlight creeping in around the doorskin silhouetting him in a golden radiance. "What say you, my kinsmen? Will you stand with me?"

His uncles and his brothers sprang to their feet and followed with him in haste to the very court of Pelias' hall.

When the king heard of them, he himself came forth to meet

them. Jason, gazing hard upon him, could see in Pelias' craggy face the marks of Tyro's beauty and in his grizzled locks the traces of her lovely hair. Indeed, this was his uncle; the people would know it, for Jason, too, had Tyro's hair. Aeson's counsel had been wise.

In a soft voice, Jason let his smooth words fall, laying for himself a wise foundation.

"Hail, Pelias, son of Poseidon of the Rock. You and I both know men's hearts leap often to sport advantage, rather than the right, finding the next day the taste wry in the mouth. I and you, descended from illustrious fathers and one noble woman, must rule our wrath and together weave our future fortunes. Each of us, facing the golden sun, know that Apollo and the Fates recoil when kin sheds kinsman's blood. This dark shame has never stained our honor. Before the gods I swear, if you swear likewise, that it never will.

"We must not reach, you and I, for the javelins or the swords of biting bronze. Your sheep and herds of tawny oxen, and all the fields on which you live, having stolen them from my parents, I yield to you. Nourish your house with them, fatten your wealth, for I care not. Give to me my father's scepter of absolute rule, the throne on which the son of Cretheus sat and gave straight judgements to a people of horsemen. I claim these from you in my father's name, and in my father's name I will rule them well. To spare both of us further sorrow, give me these, and let no fresh evil come between us!"

His words hung in the still morning, and Jason knew that he had spoken well.

Gently, too, did Pelias respond. "It shall be as you say, and let no god-offending evil come. Yet hear me, Jason. You are young, untried; I have ruled well. Let it be that you shall first give proof to the people that you are wise and capable of ruling, worthy and honorable. I am now in the sere of life, which in you only now bursts into golden flower. Phrixus is calling. Never shall his spirit rest or our people flourish until the thick-piled Fleece of the golden Ram has been returned to Iolcus. A dream has told me this, and the Oracle bids me man a ship to set out at once on the god-approved quest. But I am old. You have the power and youth to still Phrixus' wrathful spirit. Achieve this task, and I swear before Zeus, the father of both our races, that you henceforward shall be sole king in Iolcus!"

And the heart of Jason flamed within him at Pelias' guileful words, and with strong oaths he approved the covenant with firm-clasped hands.

As they parted, Jason's mind was already racing off like a swift-footed messenger, summoning all the flower of the country to his side. This was an undertaking beyond his dreams, worthy of the sons of Minyas, a feat which already he could hear being sung by the bards before uncounted hearths for generations yet unborn. The journey of Jason, the Quest of the Golden Fleece!

DEPARTURE

JASON'S CALL to high adventure echoed through all the length and breadth of that proud land.

"You who are young and brave, who would not live by your mother's side a ventureless life, who dare risk death for the fair enchantment of your own valor, hear me! A quest is afoot!" It was a call that kindled the hot blood in every youth with any pretensions to nobility or manhood.

From the mountains and the valleys they came, and from the islands, the young and even some no longer youthful. As they came, by land and sea, the stories swelled, and Jason's heart beat high to hear the bards and street musicians already singing of the great adventure. Of those singers, the sweetest was the most illustrious, Orpheus the lute-player, lord of Bistonian Pieria. It was said that the music of his voice enchanted mountain rocks and rushing streams, that he could lure the wild oaks on the coast of Thrace to march rank on serried rank. Now here he was in Iolcus, his blood on fire to sail the seas with Jason.

Orpheus sang, and the street rumors swelled. The faithful,

28

and the superstitious, murmured that Hera herself had blessed
the undertaking, that the old crone Jason had borne across the
river had been none less than she. The ship that Jason had
ordered built was rising, they whispered, under Athene's grey-
eyed gaze. Every day the people flocked to the port of Iolcus to
marvel at its grace, and every day the young heroes arrived, the
finest of sailors, the flower of golden Greece. And Jason mar-
shaled and approved them all.

Already he could envision the list of names cast into pillars
of bronze, could see himself, grey-haired and proud, recounting
them to his own awed descendants. *Orpheus. Asterion,* quickly
come from Peiresiae near Mount Phylleium. The aged *Polyphemus* from Larissa, his limbs weighted with age, but his
fighting spirit alive as in the days he fought against the cen-
taurs.

Iphiclus, Jason's own uncle, brother of Alcimede, come
through bonds of kinship. *Admetus,* wealthy sheep-raising king
of Pherae. *Erytus* and *Echion,* endowed with the guile of their
father Hermes. Their kinsman *Aethalides. Coronus,* from rich
Gyrton, Titaretsian *Mopsus,* who could read the will of the
gods in the flights of birds. From Ctimene, near the lake of
Xynia, *Eurydamas.* From Opus, *Menoetius.* His nephew *Eury-
tion;* and the valiant *Eribotes,* and the brave *Oileus.*

Clytius and *Iphitus,* brothers, and Wardens of Oechalia. *Telamon* and *Peleus,* come together for the first time since they fled
Aegina after their mad killing of their brother Phocus. From
Attica, *Butes* the battle-loving and *Phaleros* of the good ashen
spear. From Thespian Siphae, the expert mariner *Tiphys,* who
felt called to the journey by the Lady Athene herself; he could
learn from sun and star when storms were brewing and where
a ship might safely sail. From Araethyrea came *Phlias* the
wealthy son of the divine Dionysus. From Argos, the brothers
Talaus and *Areius,* and the powerful *Leodocus.*

One day there arrived a massive hot-tempered giant, whose
coming reached Jason in excited rumors even before the arrival

of the man himself. *Hercules* the hero, strongest man on earth, interrupting his labors of penance under Eurystheus, King of Mycenae, bringing with him his beloved young arms-bearer, *Hylas.*

"Came as soon as I heard the rumors," he roared, clasping Jason in an embrace of iron. "I'd just gotten back from the Erymathian swamp, had that cursed boar bellowing and snorting on my shoulders when I heard. I dropped the beast—tied up, fortunately—at the entrance to the market at Mycenae and set out. Didn't even tell Eurystheus, who no doubt turned purple. Will you have me, Jason?"

Jason knew why Hercules asked the question. His emotions, as the whole world knew, were strong and uncontrollable, and at times his rage was totally at odds with his usual good nature. During a period of madness—brought on, it was said, by Hera, who hated Hercules because he was Zeus' son—Hercules had killed his own three small sons and his beloved wife Megara. Later, when in sanity and horror he had learned what he had done, he had followed instructions of the Delphic Oracle and pledged himself in service to his cousin Eurystheus King of Mycenae, to achieve purification. Thus far he had done four great labors: choked to death the Nemean lion, which no weapons could kill; killed the nine-headed Lernean hydra, whose lopped-off heads had multiplied like rumors; captured alive the great stag sacred to Artemis; and captured the great boar by driving it, exhausted, into deep snow.

In the eyes of the world, Hercules, shedder of kinsmen's blood, was defiled and a defiler of all those who touched him. It was a point of view with which Hercules himself agreed, despite the fact he had been unconscious of his own horrid deed. But Jason was not concerned with such superstition. Hercules was strong, he was invincible, he was a man after Jason's heart. He returned Hercules' embrace enthusiastically. "With you beside me, I know we shall not fail!"

And still they came, the young heroes. *Nauplius,* descended from the Sea-God himself. *Idmon* of Argos, a son of Apollo and, like Mopsus, skilled in augury of birds; his bird-lore had told him he would die upon the quest and still he came, caring more for his honor than for life. From Sparta, *Castor* and *Pollux,* twin sons of Leda. The sons of Aphareus of Arene— *Lynceus* the keen-eyed and *Idas* the insolent, alike in strength and courage. *Periclymenus,* eldest son of Neleus king of Pylos, endowed with enormous strength. From Arcadia, *Amphidamas* and *Cepheus,* two sons of Aleus, and their nephew *Ancaeus* clad in a bearskin and brandishing a two-edged axe—his grandfather had hidden his clothes in hopes of keeping him at home.

Augeias came, the lord of the Eleans and possessor of great wealth. Fathered according to legend by the Sun, he was curious to see the Colchian king who was also sun-descended. *Asterius* and his brother *Amphion* came from Achaean Hellene; and from Taenarum, *Euphemus,* world's fastest runner, son of Europa and the god Poseidon. And two more excellent seamen, fathered according to legend by Poseidon: *Erginus* of Miletus, and *Ancaeus,* the proud, of Samos. From Calydon, *Meleager,* the young and valiant, and his uncles *Laocoon* and *Iphiclus. Palaemus,* the lame but manly, son it was said of Hephaestus, the lame blacksmith god. *Iphitus* of Phocis, who had been Jason's host when Jason consulted the Pythian oracle.

From the wintry land of Thrace swiftly came *Zetes* and *Calais,* sons of the North Wind. Glints of gold spangles shone among the dusky feathers of the wings they wore upon their ankles, cloaks of scarlet feathers ruffled upon their backs, and their black hair streamed in the dark wind.

Of this caliber and number were the nobles, brave and mostly young, who poured into Iolcus at the call of Jason, son of Aeson. As they came, the townspeople stared in wonder, and the rumors swelled. Soon a name arose among the people for this company of young lords. *Minyae . . .* sons of Minyas. That great hero, King of Thessaly, had been ancestor of all the greatest of these venturers. Alcimede's mother, Clymene, had been one of Minyas' daughters, and from the first moment Jason heard the name whispered in the streets, he liked it well.

All was ready. The great ship, called the *Argo,* was complete, equipped with all that was needful for business across the seas. At last the day dawned. Long before Apollo's chariot climbed the sky, the streets were alive with watchers, well-wishers and whisperers. Jason, donning his shining armor by Aeson's hearth-fire, had heard the whispers. The doorskin was looped back, and he could see his fellow venturers hurrying by, making their way to the shore called Magnesian Pagasae, where the *Argo* lay. The young lords shone among the eager people like bright stars in a cloudy sky. On either side, women lifted up hands to heaven, praying to the gods for their safe return.

The women had been weeping, and to Jason's annoyance Alcimede had heard their words. "Poor Alcimede, to taste such calamity so late in life. . . ." "Poor Aeson, better he should have been long since in the grave than to lose so soon a new-found son . . ." "The expedition is ill-starred . . ." "Ill-starred. . . ." And the men's voices, in grave counter-chorus: "Lord Zeus, what does Pelias do?" "It is exile or death he is wishing on this band of noble men . . ." "The journey is unsafe, the going hard . . ."

Alcimede clung to Jason's neck, her eyes bright with tears. Around them, women and servants had caught the mood and were overcome with grief. Jason was impatient; more, he was angry. To have this moment, this supreme hour, dimmed and muffled with despair! Then his brow cleared. No matter! Think of the celebration and joy on his return, the greater because none but he himself had believed the day would come! His one concern at the moment was his father, Aeson. Age had fallen on him swiftly and now he lay, wrapped against the chill, like a figure cut in stone. Would Aeson live to see the triumph of return?

I must not think of that, Jason told himself. My men are waiting. He spoke to the household with reassuring words, intended mainly for Aeson's ears. Then he turned to his young pages. "My equipment. Take it, and go."

They obeyed in silence, their eyes upon the ground. Clearly, they thought they were setting towards their deaths. The attendants and friends, casting a glance at Aeson and Alcimede, took their leave, leaving parents and son to make farewells in private.

Alcimede held Jason still tight in her arms, weeping in black despair. "Why, why did I not die the very day Pelias uttered that evil proclamation? Then I might have been buried by my son's dear hands. I that have stood as high as any woman in the land am left like a servant in an empty house, pining in misery for my first and last, my only son!"

Jason disengaged her gently. "Mother, I beg you, don't. Your tears will save me nothing. We cannot know what the gods may have in store. You, like I, must endure with fortitude. Take courage! The omens and the oracles bode well. Remember what a noble company stands with me. Now stay here quietly, and be no bird of ill-omen for my bright ship."

In the moment of silence he left the house, and the doorskin dropped shut behind him.

Once in the streets, the air of the grey morning filled his lungs and lifted high his spirits. As one man, the people hailed him, and he moved through them like Apollo issuing from the fragrant shrine of Delos. As he passed the Temple of Artemis, guardian of the city, the aged priestess Iphias came forward, seizing his right hand, covering it with kisses. Jason thought that she would speak, but the crowd swept him on and Jason saw her left there by the roadside, as the old are ever bypassed by the young.

At last the well-made streets of the city lay behind him. Ahead lay the beach of Pagasae, and the great *Argo,* and his friends, awaiting in a body, their hands raised high in welcome. Jason paused a moment to collect his mind on how to first address them. Then, to his surprise, there came a shout from behind him, and thundering feet. The company ahead milled in wonder, pointing to something beyond Jason up the road. He whirled.

Down onto the beach leaped two unexpected figures. The first was Argus, builder of the ship. The other—Jason caught his breath. He had seen the youth that day in the king's palace, and Admatus had whispered his identity: Acastus, son of Pelias! Obviously they had come in haste, and secrecy, in defiance of the king's own orders.

"We are coming with you," Acastus panted. "I have no wish to be left behind from such a journey!" He gestured to his fine new double cloak. "A gift for good fortune from my sister Pelopeia."

The shipbuilder had thrown over his shoulders the hide of a great black bull, which made him look like some messenger from the underworld. Each carried a bundle, tied hastily with cords, and had a weapon thrust through his girdle. Jason's mind teemed with questions, but here was neither time nor place. Turning to the company he bade them seat themselves for conference.

In rows they sat, on the furled sail and the long mast lying on the pebbled sand, and they turned themselves toward Jason.

In a friendly tone, Jason began the speech he had carefully thought out. "The ship is ready, fitted as a ship should be for a great undertaking. Given a good wind, we could sail at once. But one thing is yet to be done. Is yet for you to do." His eyes roved the alert, listening faces. "Friends . . . we are all partners and equals in this journey, partners in the return for which we hope. Therefore it lies with you now to choose our leader. I urge you, choose with no partiality, choose the best among us, for much will depend on him. He it is who must choose, when we reach Colchis, whether to deal with the foreigners as enemies or friends."

Jason stopped and waited. As one person, the eyes of the

young men turned to Hercules, as one voice they called upon
him where he sat at center. Hercules, to Jason's astonishment,
did not move. He raised his right hand, saying "I will not accept this honor, nor will I let any other among you rise to it.
No one must lead us but the one who gathered us together."

Thus Hercules the generous repaid Jason who had welcomed
him stained with the guilt of blood, and his words won the
applause and acceptance of the company. And the heart of
Jason leapt high within him.

Eagerly he rose again to his feet. "If indeed you do entrust
me with this honor, let us at once make ready. Enough delays!
The time has come for sacrifice and feasting. Oxen are coming.
While we wait, let us launch the ship into the water. Let us load
our gear, and cast lots for our places at the oars. And let us
build an altar to Apollo, lord of journey's beginnings, for he
has promised me through his oracles that he will guide and
counsel us in our seafaring."

Jason himself was the first to begin the work at hand, and
the others leaped to follow his example, stripping off their garments and piling them on a high smooth ledge of rock. Super-
vised by the shipbuilder, they girded the *Argo* with strong rope
that her planks might stand any pounding of the seas. Swiftly
they hollowed a runway in the sand, wide as the *Argo*'s beam,
far into the sea as the prow would reach in launching. Deeper
and deeper they dug the trench as it advanced. Smooth rollers
from the trunks of trees they laid along her bottom and, this
done, they tipped the great ship down on the first rollers.

High on both sides of the ship, the oars were swung inward,
each handle fastened to its pin so that a good grip for a man's
two hands projected outward. Tiphys leaped on board, and the
young men formed in ranks on either side, each breasting an
oar and pressing with his hands. At Tiphys' mighty shout, they
leaned all weight upon the task. Their first heave shifted the
Argo from her beachhead; feet straining forward, they kept her
on the move. Swiftly, between the twin lines of shouting men,

Argo ran to the sea's embrace. From the groaning rollers, rubbed by the weighty keel, rose a great pall of smoke. Pelian *Argo* was as eager to be off as a young girl running to her first lover, and her guardians had to stand fast, checking her with hawsers.

Joyously in the midday sun, the young lords fitted the oars properly into the holes and loaded the stores, the mast and the well-made sail. Then, when all was ready, they cast lots among them for their paired places at the oars. But for the midships seat they cast no lots, they gave that bench to Hercules and chose as his mate Ancaeus of the two-edged axe, and they left that bench to their sole use. Likewise the young lords agreed with one voice that none but Tiphys, greatest of sailors, should be their helmsman. This time, Hercules did not protest, and Jason heard and was silent, but his brain thought many thoughts.

Now the ship was launched, and the time had come for prayer and dedication. By the shore, shingles were piled into an altar for Apollo, god of shores and embarkations. Quickly on top were laid logs of olive wood. Two oxen had arrived, driven by herdsmen, and the youngest of the young lords dragged the animals forward while the others made ready the water and the barleycorns. Then Jason called upon Apollo, lord of his ancestors.

"Apollo, Lord of the Sun, you who dwell in Pagasae and in Aesonis, city of my father's name; you who did promise to guide me through this journey, hear me! You it is who have caused my undertaking; to you I look for a safe journey and a safe return. Then once again will we glorify your altar, one bull for each mariner safe returned, and other gifts without number also will I give you. Accept now the sacrifice we offer you as payment for our safe passage, first of the sacrifices we will make for *Argo*. May your will bring me luck as I cast off; may weather fair and breezes gentle carry us across the unknown sea. Come, Archer-King!"

Jason sprinkled the barleycorns upon the altar. Now Ancaeus
and Hercules stepped forward. Hercules swung his club, striking one of the oxen full on the brow, and the mighty animal
sank to the ground forthwith. In like manner Ancaeus, with
his axe of bronze, smote the other oxen's neck, severing the
great sinews, and forward it pitched onto its horns. Then their
companions sprang to slit the beasts' throats, to flay them, and
to carve the flesh. The sacred pieces from the thighs were
wrapped in fat and burned upon the faggots. Jason poured out
the offering of unwatered wine.

Idmon the augurer watched intently as the bright flames
sprang round the offering, and the smoke rose in dark spirals,
promising good fortune. Idmon spoke at once, and clearly, telling Apollo's mind.

"The gods and the Fates decree your safe return, here to this
place and bearing the sacred Fleece, though many trials await
you on the way. I myself will not return. I have long known
that I am doomed to die in Asia. Nonetheless I have come, that
in my homeland I may be remembered as one who sailed in
Argo."

This was all he spoke, and young lords listening were filled
at once with mingled grief and joy.

Now the sun had begun to throw the shadows of rocks across
the fields. The young lords, the Minyae, strewed the sand thick
with leaves and lay down upon them in rows above the surf.
Beside them were appetizing foods and mellow wine, servants
to keep them plentifully supplied, all the pleasures of Dionysus,
god of fellowship and wine. Soon, like young men well content
at a pleasant banquet, their voices rose in gallant tales.

Only Jason withdrew into himself to brood upon his troubles.

Soon Idas noticed and called out in a loud voice. "Jason,
what's the matter with you? Why these deep thoughts? Does
your resolution fail? Panic often leaves a coward dumb. Now
hear me swear! By my sharp spear, which has helped me more
than Zeus himself and has won me the highest honors in war,

I swear! Nothing shall fail, no venture shall prove fatal with me beside you! No, not even if a god should rise against us!"

He lifted a brimming beaker of wine with both his hands and drank until his dark beard was drenched with the sweet wine. All the company cried out, but it was Idmon who rose and sharply spoke.

"Your words bring death, and may you be the first to suffer! You are always bold, but now this strong wine has also made you blind. There are ways to put heart in a man without offering insult to the gods!" And he cited to Idas blunt examples of how other mortals who had blasphemed had been struck down.

The insolent Idas laughed loudly, shooting Idmon an evil glance. "Use your second sight and tell me how, if I be punished, you yourself will get away alive!"

His voice was angry, and Idmon's muscles tensed, but before he could reply their companions interrupted with loud protestations, and Jason himself spoke. It was Orpheus, however, who really prevented the quarrel from turning ugly. Leaping to his feet, he raised his lyre in his left hand and began to sing.

Orpheus sang of the creation of the world, of the Age of Chaos before earth and sky were parted into separate bodies, man and wife; he sang of the creation and appointed stations of the sun, the moon and stars; of how the mountains rose, and the murmuring streams ran from the mountains down into the sea. He sang of Father Uranus and Mother Gaea, from whom all life came; of Cronos and Rhea and the Titanic Age; the fall of the Titans, the Cyclops and the Hecatonchieres of the hundred arms, and last, of the coming of Zeus the Almighty and the glorious gods who watched the deeds of all men from snow-clad Olympus.

The song was over. The lyre and the heavenly voice ceased and were still. Yet in the caressing darkness no man moved. Their heads were bent forward, their ears still filled with the ghost of Orpheus' magical song. Presently they stirred, and mixed the wine and water according to the ritual, and poured the libation on the burning tongues of flame, and yielded themselves to sleep.

When the bright eyes of dawn fell on the towering peaks of Pelion, and the headlands washed by the seas stood sharp and clear, Tiphys roused the young lords. "Come! We must embark and set the oars."

Drowsily they stirred themselves, clinging to the visions brought by sleep. Then, in the rosy stillness of the dawn, came a sound that filled them all with awe and wonder, a magical cry from the Pagasaean sea. Tiphys raised his hand. "Listen!" he said quietly. "*Argo* herself is calling."

One followed another, the young men waded into the golden sea and took their seats on the rowing benches, each in his allotted place, his equipment beside him. On the midship seat, Ancaeus sat beside Hercules' mighty bulk. Tiphys took his appointed position at the helm. At his signal, the hawsers were cast off, and the libations of wine and water poured into the waiting sea. Then, as one breath, firm arms gripped the oars and swung them strongly, and the *Argo* glided like a proud bird over the gilded waves.

Jason looked at the rich land falling away behind them. He thought of the father and mother so newly found, so quickly lost. Of Chiron the wise teacher, to whom he had not thought to return for a last farewell. And Jason turned his eyes away from the land and wept.

THE
VOYAGE
OF *ARGO*

II

THE LEMNIAN
WOMEN

NOT SO were the thoughts of the other lords as the ship put out to sea. At the stern Tiphys lifted high a cup of gold, calling on Zeus, the Father of Heavens, for a fair wind to Colchis, days gilded with sunlight, and at the last a sweet road home. And from the clouds there rolled back to him the voice of thunder. Lightning tore the sky. While Jason brooded, the young lords took new courage from the damp fresh air, believing the omens of the god. Idmon the augurer called out to them, "Fall to the oars!" and they responded, finding in his words sweet hope.

The oars struck the storm-swept sea insatiably, to the rhythm of Orpheus' lyre. The men rowed in unison as if they were dancing around Apollo's altars. Eagerly the prow of *Argo* cut through the dark salt waves. The waters, swallowing the oars, broke into angry foam. Then the storm died, and the sun shone, and the armor of the seamen gleamed like fire. All the while, a great train of foam, a long white wake, followed the ship and showed against the wine-dark sea like a fresh-furrowed path across a verdant plain. And the gods of heaven watched the young lords' passing.

While still in sight of harbor and the curving shore of Pagasae, *Argo* was rowed by her crew, and guided by her polished steering-oar, held in Tiphys' skillful hands. At his signal, as they reached deep water, the tall mast was raised in its box and made fast. Then the great sail was hauled up and unfurled, and a shrill wind welcomed it. *Argo* sailed effortlessly along the Tisaean coast while Orpheus played his lyre. He sang of Artemis, saver of ships and guardian goddess of the land of Iolcus. From the salt-sea depths fish darted to gambol in the wake, drawn by the music as sheep are drawn home at twilight by a shepherd's piping reed. And the wind, ever freshening, carried the *Argo* ever farther from the rich Pelasgian land.

Presently his kinsman Acastus called to the somber Jason. "Were you not reared near Pelion? We pass there now." Jason raised his head and turned toward the green shore, and his heart started. There was Chiron, come down from the high land, wading into the grey sea and waving his great hand. Beside him stood his wife, Chariclo, holding in her arms a small child—the infant Achilles, son of Peleus, whom she held high to wish safe journey to his father. And Jason took new heart and his spirits rose.

The Cape of Sepian came into view, and lay behind, then Sciathus, girded by the seas. Then, far ahead under the clear skies, appeared the main Magnesian coast. And the wind veered against them, so they beached their ship as darkness fell. There by night, on the shore, they sacrificed a sheep, while behind them the sea beat high against the rocks. For two days they rested, but on the third, as they rose at dawn, Tiphys' voice called.

"The wind has changed!" And they hoisted the great sail and again put out to sea.

Past Meliboea's stormy beaches *Argo* forged, and the next sunrise past Homole slanting down to the sea. Soon the river Amyrus lay behind, and Eurymenae, and Ossa's and Olympus' deep ravines. All day and all night they ran before the wind, to

Pallene, to Cape Canastra where the hills rise high. And in the rosy dawn the peak of Mount Athos raised a finger to the sky. All that day and night a stiff breeze stretched the sail. But with the first rays of the following dawn the wind died, and there came a calm, and the men took to the oars. All day they rowed, and as day waned they found themselves at a rocky isle.

"A good place to beach," Tiphys commented. "Perhaps by morning the wind will come again."

Jason rubbed his aching shoulders. "What people live here?"

"The Lemnians, under Thoas, their king."

"Friendly?"

"Not towards the Thracians. The Thracian men, that is. Rumor has it that among the Lemnian men there is an over-fondness for the Thracian women."

"Here comes a welcoming party," said a voice behind Jason's shoulder.

"Welcoming? Look at the armor and the weapons."

"No army. Look at them," Idas said contemptuously. "A rabble, milling in panic." Then, his voice changed to that of one stunned by a great stone. "By the god of war! They're women!"

All of them, women. Pouring through the gates of Myrine like ravening Maenads, of all ages, all sizes. Girt with ill-fitting armor and dragging heavy weapons, they streamed onto the beach, staring out at the great-prowed ship. Jason stared back. "By Aphrodite," he breathed, fascinated, "no men! No men at all."

As he gazed, a new figure appeared through the Myrine gate. For a moment, before he laughed off his own superstition, the thought flared in Jason's mind that his oath had summoned the goddess herself. Not in fear like the others did this woman move, but proudly, despite the swiftness with which her slender sandalled feet carried her down onto the beach. She wore, above her white robes, a kingly armor cast in bronze, but she stood tall, disdaining its great weight. And she was young, and very fair.

Jason motioned to Aethalides, never taking his own eyes from the slim golden figure. "Go ashore, with your father Hermes' own speed. Persuade the ladies we come in peace to spend the night."

Swiftly Aethalides went, and swiftly did return. "The lady Hypsipyle, daughter of Thoas, grants that we may stay."

And the Argonauts cast anchor and slept that night upon the shore. In the morning came a fair breeze from the north, but they did not sail.

Jason lingered, and so did the others too, laughing among themselves and casting covert glances towards the barred Myrenian gate. Just when at last, reluctantly, they began to pack their gear and move toward the water, the gate opened, and Jason called upon the men to halt.

The woman that came towards them was not the fair Amazon he had seen the night before. But she too was young and walked among them gracefully without fear. Jason went to meet her.

She met him as warriors meet who are equal in strength and honor. "The lady Hypsipyle bids me invite your captain to come to the palace to hear from her our people's will. I am to tell you it will please you well. For all the rest, you all are welcome if you wish to come into the town as friends."

This seemed to Jason a welcome fit and proper, and he was pleased that his shipmates urged him to depart at once and prepared themselves to follow.

But not immediately did Jason leave. First he stripped off his clothes and bathed himself in the morning sea. Next he donned his saffron trousers. And around his shoulders he fastened a wondrous cloak. Of crimson cloth, made doubly wide by borders of royal purple, it outshone in brilliance the splendor of the rising sun.

Here in embroidery of curious design were the Cyclops, hammering out an everlasting thunderbolt for Zeus the King. Here were the sons of Antiope, building the town of Thebes. Here was long-haired Aphrodite, wielding the bronze shield of her lover Ares; her tunic had slipped from her shoulder to reveal her lovely breast, and her beauty was mirrored perfectly in the bronze.

Here also was the woodland pasture grazed by oxen, the dewy grass stained with the blood of fighting raiders and herdsmen. Here was the chariot-race between Pelops and Oenamaus, with Oenamaus, spear lifted, just spilling out of the chariot as the axle twisted and broke. Here was the youth Apollo, shooting an arrow at the giant Tityos who was abducting his mother Leto. And here also was Phrixus the Minyan, shown vividly with the Ram of the Golden Fleece.

Such was the cloak that Jason wore as he set out for Hypsipyle. In his right hand he held a spear, given him by the warlike Atalanta, who would have sailed with him on *Argo* had Jason let her. Eagerly Jason strode towards the Myrenian gate, his gold hair down his shoulders, looking like the bright star of dawn. As he entered the gates, the women flocked after him, but he walked resolutely, his eyes upon the ground, until he reached the royal palace. There the fine-paneled double doors were fast thrown open, and the girl Iphinoe, who had been the messenger, appeared and led Jason quickly through the rich-appointed hall, to a polished chair.

There Jason sat, and now he raised his eyes, to the face of the lady Hypsipyle. And it was Hypsipyle who blushed and looked away.

The voice of Hypsipyle was honey-sweet.

"Stranger, why have you stayed outside the gates of our city that has lost its men? For our men have left us; I will tell you the whole sorry truth; they have deserted our land and our women to plow the fields of Thrace."

Jason's gaze upon her was calculated to communicate what fools he deemed these men, and she blushed again.

"Hear me, stranger. In the days when my father Thoas ruled, our men used to sail in raids upon the Thracian farmsteads.

They brought home prizes, and they brought home women. Aphrodite, that fickle goddess, took from those men all sense of right and wrong. They looked with loathing on their wedded wives; they turned from their homes; they indulged their passions with the captive women. Still we endured this, hoping for a change of heart. But the evil spread. Lawful children were left to starve, a bastard generation grew, unmarried girls were left to wander, No son, no father, no brother protected us or thought of aught but the captive girls. At last our minds were filled with desperate resolution. When the men next went to Thrace, we shut the city gates against them. Upon their return they begged from us all male children in the city, and they went back to Thrace, where now they live.

"With the dawn today, we women met in council. We have resolved to accommodate you strangers with food and wine, for it is ever better to give than to be robbed. But more, we have bethought our future welfare. You came here unannounced; so might the Thracians or our other enemies. Moreover, the old and wise among us die, but no children come. Who, in time, will yoke the oxen, will watch the changing seasons for the times to sow and reap? Who will be left to bury us when we grow old? So we have determined to hold out to you an invitation. Stay here and settle with us. If the prospect pleases you and you accept, the scepter of my royal father shall be yours."

So she spoke, and her eyes, meeting Jason's promised even more. Jason's blood raced, but he made politic answer.

"Gracious lady, we need your aid. Everything you would give us will be welcome. I shall return to the ship to tell my people all that you have said. But I must leave the royal scepter in your hand. Not through indifference! I am vowed to a perilous adventure, which calls me on."

As he spoke, he touched her right hand. Then quickly he turned and left, and as he went, numberless young girls danced round him, escorting him to the city gates.

Jason reported to his comrades all that Hypsipyle had spoken, and when he was through they beheld the fairest of the girls driving down the beach in sweet-running wagons filled with gifts. They found no difficulty in inducing the Argonauts to go with them to their homes . . . all but Hercules, who chose to remain behind with a few of his favorite friends.

And Jason himself returned to Hypsipyle's palace. The city came alive with dance and music, with banquet and with wine, and the torches burned, and the scent of burnt offerings perfumed the air. The offerings burned to Hephaestus, god of fire, and his consort Aphrodite the Cyprian, goddess of desire. One by one the torches guttered and went out, and soft night blanketed the sky, and when rosy-fingered dawn peered over the horizon Jason still lay in Hypsipyle's arms.

Day followed day, and the breeze blew fair, and the ship *Argo* lay in harbor like a bride forsaken by her bridegroom. At last Hercules cast down his giant club and strode ashore. Grimly he walked the city, calling out the men, summoning them to a meeting on the beach. He shut the gates firm shut against the women and turned upon his friends.

"Good my lords, I ask you, why are we here? Are our women at home so ugly we have come for brides? Where are our bright oaths and our great hopes for glory? We will find none by plowing the fields of Lemnos, I do assure you. It's no use praying the gods for a miracle. The Fleece will not come home to Greece of its own accord. If we sail not to Colchis, let us return to our own homes, and leave our leader here in Hypsipyle's arms to achieve renown by repopulating Lemnos!"

Not one man among them could look Hercules in the eye. No more was said. They rose and hastened to make preparations for departure.

Meanwhile the women, shut out from their counsels, watched and waited, for their apprehensions were aroused. Soon the import of the Argonauts' intention came to them on the wind, and they swarmed to the Gates, and came running down onto the beach with moans of grief. They came as bees come pouring from the hive when the meadows sparkle with the dew. To each of the young lords they came with tears and with loving embraces and kind words and prayers for their safe return.

And Lemnian Hypsipyle herself came down, her tears streaming like her golden hair, to hold for the last time the hands of the lover she was losing.

"Go," she whispered. "May the gods bring you and all your companions safely home. And may you win the Fleece of Gold that holds your heart. This island and this scepter I will hold for you, if ever you should choose to come again. Somehow my heart knows this is not to be. Nonetheless, remember me when you are far away. And tell me what you wish me to do if the gods allow me to bear your son."

Jason was moved by her gracious words. "Hypsipyle, do not think ill of me if I choose to live in my own land. And may the happy gods grant your prayers for my safe journey. But if that is not my destiny and if you bear my son, send him when he is old enough to Iolcus, to comfort my aged parents and care for them if they are yet alive."

With that, Jason disengaged his hands and went on board, and the young lords followed, each to his allotted seat, and manned the oars. Argus the shipbuilder loosed the ropes that held *Argo* to the sea-beat rock, and the oarsmen struck the water with the oars.

Hypsipyle stood upon the dock, her arm raised high, her bright hair like a fleece of gold, but Jason did not look back.

ISLE OF
THE DOLIONES

THAT NIGHT they beached at Samothrace. This was the isle of Electra, Atlas' daughter, a place of secret rites, and it was the wish of Orpheus that by holy initiation in these rituals the Argonauts might sail with heightened confidence over the awesome sea. And so they did, but of these secret rituals we may not sing.

Next, eagerly rowing, they moved over the Gulf of Melas betwixt the land of Thrace and the land of Imbros, and at sunset to the shore of the Chersonese. There they encountered a strong south wind, and they gave to it the great sail and sped by night through the dark, swirling Hellespont, named for Athamas' lost daughter.

There is an island in the Propontis that slopes steeply to the sea. It is parted from the rich mainland only by a narrow isthmus, east of the River Aesepus, and the inhabitants of its mountain are a fierce and lawless tribe. But the isthmus and the fertile plain belonged to Cyzicus the noble, king of the Doliones. Here, in a stiff breeze from Thrace, *Argo* came, and entered into the harbor called Fairhaven. And Cyzicus and the

Doliones welcomed the Argonauts with hospitality, inviting them to moor in the city harbor. And so they did, building an altar on the beach to Apollo, god of happy landings. Cyzicus himself supplied the sheep and the good wine for the sacrifice. He had been told by an oracle to expect the coming of such a noble band, and to greet them with no show of arms. He, too was young, and he resembled Jason. He, too had not yet known the joys of fatherhood. Indeed, he had but lately wed the gentle lady Cleite, paying for her a kingly bride price. But generously he left her in their bridal chamber and dined instead with Jason. Jason told him the story of their noble quest, and Cyzicus shared with him his knowledge of the broad Propontic Gulf, which they had now to sail.

When morning came, Jason turned to a few chosen companions. "Let us climb to the top of Dindymum and see if we can see the waters we must cross. Cyzicus could tell us nothing beyond the Propontic Gulf." He did not mean to sound patronizing, but he knew at once from the look on some faces that his thoughts must have showed. It did seem odd that Cyzicus, intelligent and noble, had never himself scaled Bear Mountain for such survey.

Hercules nodded. "Go. And I and the rest will bring *Argo* into harbor—and stay there ready in case you again need rescuing."

"Rescuing!" Jason swung around.

"Aye. In case you again find your Golden Fleece attached to a living female."

"It might have been better had you come ashore yourself at Lemnos, instead of lingering on shipboard with Hylas and your favorite youths!" Jason's voice warmed with the memory, "The inhabitants were most friendly."

"And could in time have proved most unfriendly, as they did to their own lawful mates."

"Hypsipyle told us of that," Jason said hotly. "And I consider they behaved most honorably to dishonorable men."

"She told you not quite all. The women did not shut out their men, they butchered them—every infant, boy and man, and their foreign whores!" Hercules snapped. "All except the king; his daughter was too nice to butcher him, so she sent him out to sea in a wooden chest in hopes he'd wash ashore somewhere, as it seems he did. We were not quite alone on shipboard, Jason; we had some visitors, who apparently brought us more truth than you. It's a lesson it might be well for you to remember, mighty leader. This is how women can befuddle you. And how they reward those who betray their love."

"The sun is rising," Telamon put in hastily. "Let us choose our men and leave before the heat comes heavy on the mountain." And Jason, wisely considering Hercules' strength, allowed himself to be persuaded.

As always, the physical exertion and the sheer delight in his own prowess gradually drove the black anger from Jason's mind, and he was visited with exhilaration and a surge of joy. When they stood on the mountain, the hot sun beating down and beads of sweat standing out upon their rippling muscles, he grinned at his companions in speechless comradeship. Below them, glittering like jewels, spread the panorama—rivers and mountains, sea and fertile plain. And far ahead, beyond the mist-wreathed peaks, Colchis of the Unfriendly Sea.

"One day," Jason thought, "one day I shall stand like this looking down on Iolcus, and know that it is mine."

Telamon touched his shoulder. "The others will be waiting. Come."

Jason turned, nodding. Then, as he squinted down at the way which he had come, he swore and stiffened. "Look!"

Far below, like toys, they lay—the ship, the harbor, the miniature men. Only from the other side round the mountain, other figures swarmed. Savages, clothed in skins, seeming more beasts than men, sending great boulders crashing down into the harbor to pen the Argonauts like animals in a trap. Pelting Hercules and his swift-pulled bow with jagged rocks. With cries of fury, Jason and his companions, their mission forgot, charged down into the fray. The monsters turned and charged, but the young lords were armed with spears and arrows, and in the end they killed them all.

Like axe-hewn timbers the fallen monsters looked, stretched on the grey stones of the harbor beach. A sprawling mass, some with feet on the sands and eyes and gaping mouths open to salt sea water; others reversed, their faces deep in sand. No identity, no dignity, carrion for fish and birds. And Jason looked, and laughed, for the day was his.

They boarded ship, loosed hawsers, and under Tiphys' directions the great sail caught the breeze. All day they sailed ahead through choppy seas. With dusk the wind began to fail. Then suddenly it veered; it rose into a gale; it sent them scudding into the unknown dark. Men clung to their oars, and swore, and prayed, if they believed in prayer, to their favorite gods. Jason grabbed at Tiphys, but that trained sailor, intent upon his steering, flung him off. "Leave be! There's land ahead. I'm going to try to get us into shore."

"Where are we?"

"The gods alone know. Now stand off!"

Tensely, under Tiphys' guidance, they reached shore and made fast the hawsers to the rocks. Night's dark mantle lay upon the land, so they could not see more than to make camp around a small, weak fire. Then suddenly, out of the dark, armed figures circled.

Jason sprang to his feet, seizing his spears. "Attack!"

They were surrounded by the land's inhabitants, taking them for raiders. And Jason's companions were not slow to their own defense. Shield clashed on shield, and ashen spear on spear. Like forest fire, meeting dry brush and leaping up, the two bands met and plunged each other into the horror of war.

The attackers were valiant, but they were no match for Hercules, nor for Acastus and Peleus, Idas and Clytius, Castor and Pollux and Meleager, nor for Telamon with his great ashen spear. Jason himself struck down their leader, smiting full upon the breast so that his spear shattered the warrior's bone. As the man sank down upon the sand like a trapped bird, the rest gave way in panic, like doves before a hawk. They rushed wildly for the gates as Jason lifted his voice in a roar of triumph that was soon echoed by lamentations from far off in the darkness behind the city's walls. Then the country was still, and Jason and his companions lay down to sleep beside their fire.

Night passed; dawn came, and Jason rose to look upon the field of the fallen. He looked and was struck dumb with horror. The land on which he stood was the very land, which the morn before they had left. There at his feet lay the bodies of the noblest of his Dolione hosts, the stalwart Gephyrus, Itymoneus the dauntless, and Artaces, that dashing soldier. And more beside them—Jason walked among them until he came to the man he had killed, and his heart became numb with grief. There in the dust and blood he beheld Cyzicus the young king, twin to himself in looks and valor. Cyzicus the brave and noble and newly wed.

The other Minyae silently awoke, and rose, and were overcome with the sight they saw. They chose the noblest among them to go up into the city under a black flag in solemn mourning. In like manner the Doliones came forth to meet them, and for three days the Minyae and Doliones together mourned and wailed and tore their hair. Then, three times, together, wearing their bronze armor, they marched round the dead king and laid him in his tomb. And together they raised a barrow on the grey plain to the memory of Cyzicus, King of the Doliones, and round it they held the customary funeral games.

Nor was this the end of their sorrow. The gentle lady Cleite, bride of Cyzicus, took a rope and hanged herself by the neck until she was dead. Never had such a day of horror come to the Doliones. Not one among them, man or woman, could bear to eat.

The weather, sharing the sorrow, was foul by day and night,

so the Argonauts could not put out to sea. But towards the end of the thirteenth night, Mopsus, who with Acastus had been standing watch, waked Jason where he lay wrapped comfortably in fleece.

"My lord, while you slept a halcyon hovered above your head and piped an omen. This peak of Dindymum is the throne of Rhea, the dread Earth-Mother. You must climb to the holy summit in propitiation, and the storms will cease."

Jason leaped up, rejoicing. Hastily he woke the others and told them of how Mopsus had read the sea-bird's signs. At once they set to work. The youngest unloosed oxen from their stalls and began to drive them up the steep mountain path. The others rowed *Argo* into anchorage; then they, too, followed, leaving only a handful of men to guard the ship.

From the peak they could see the whole length of the coast of Thrace, close enough to touch it seemed, and far off lay the entrance to the Bosphorus, wreathed in mists. In the woods they found an ancient vine withered to the roots of its massive trunk. Of this Argus the carver made a sacred image to Rhea the Great Mother, and this they set on the rocks in the shelter of oaks, the tallest trees that grow. They made an altar of small stones and, crowning themselves with oak leaves, began the sacrifice.

Jason himself poured the wine upon the blaze, earnestly begging Rhea to send the storms away. Led by Orpheus, the young men in their bronze armor moved round the altar, stepping high in dance. They beat their swords upon their shields to drown out the wails of grief still rising from the city far below. And the goddess must have observed their sacrifice with pleasure, for the trees shed fruit abundantly, the earth showed tender grass, the beasts of the woodlands left their lairs and came forth with wagging tails, and a pure spring gushed out for them from the mountaintop. And the young lords feasted on the mountain and sang in honor of the ancient goddess.

By dawn the wind had stilled. The young lords came down

in triumph from the mountain and swarmed onto *Argo* to the rowing seats. The still air had put the waves to sleep, the sea was calm, and the Minyae rejoiced, for they were seized with a spirit of rivalry. Willingly they fell to the oars, each trying to outlast the other in endurance. And to the sound of their joyous singing, *Argo* sped from harbor, and the Dolionian sorrow lay behind them and was forgotten.

HYLAS

AT FIRST they rowed so swiftly that not even Poseidon's whirlwind horses could have passed them. But as the day wore on, strong winds swept down from the rivers, roughening the sea, and the men wearied, and their efforts slackened. Only Hercules still labored at full strength, the pull of his great arms making the whole ship shudder. And the others, shamed in their exhaustion, gritted their teeth and pulled with him.

Tiphys peered ahead across the choppy sea, his brow furrowed.

"Where now?" Jason queried.

"Only passing the mouth of the Rhyndacus. We need to make the coast of Mysia by dusk."

Around him, scarcely muffled, there were groans. Hercules turned and glared. "What ails you, you pack of women! Afraid of a good day's labor? Very well!" He gripped his own stout oar in both his fists and strained to it, grinding it into the water as if he were a field hand plowing furrows in a stony field. For three sweeps of the great pine, the others sat and

watched. Then suddenly there was a crack like mighty thunder.
"By holy Hades!" Hercules' astonished voice bellowed.

None knew quite how it had happened, but there was
the oar being swept away in the grey waves. There on the
floor of *Argo*, fallen off his seat like a scuffling child, was
the giant Hercules, staring blankly at the broken handle in
his hands.

Unwisely, a few allowed themselves to laugh. Hercules sat
up, speechless with fury. For once, however, that fury could
be turned on no one but himself, a fact they all enjoyed. Like
a hobbled ox, he lumbered back to his bench, where he sat con-
templating his idle hands in silence.

Even without Hercules, they made the Mysian shore by sup-
pertime. Jason, looking at the bearlike giant, bit back a smile.
Hercules, his oar departed, was helpless and sullen with en-
forced inactivity. As the other Argonauts reached the shore
and began to set about their camping preparations, Hercules
stomped off into the forest. At first he moved with seeming
aimlessness but soon he stopped, deliberating, before a young
pine with a trunk like a slender poplar. Down on the ground
went the bow and arrows, and the Nemean lionskin of which
he was so proud, and he began to belabor the trunk with his
bronze-studded club while Jason, amused, stood watching.

"Better he wears out his anger on a tree than on us," was
Jason's first thought. Then his humor changed to reluctant
admiration as Hercules spread his great legs, pressed his shoulder against the pine and, seizing it by the roots in both massive
hands, began to shake it as a dog will shake a rat. Forward,
backward, forward, and again back and with a mighty wrench
the tree came, clots and all, out of the ground. The force threw
Hercules backward, but Jason dared not laugh. Undaunted the
giant rose, slung the pine upon his shoulder and, collecting his
gear, started matter-of-factly back towards the shore.

Jason, meeting him casually, thought it prudent not to inquire
his purpose. But Hercules' mood had shifted as suddenly as

summer weather. "New oar," he said pleasantly. "Seemed the best thing to get at it right away."

"Where's your young shadow?"

"Hylas?" Hercules' voice softened. "Gone for water. For the evening meal, and probably for me to bathe. The boy seems to think I ought to more often."

"He's a good servant."

"A good lad," Hercules corrected, the affection evident in his voice. "A prince, you know. Had him since he was a child, ever since I had to kill his father."

Jason kept silent. Hylas' father, the Dryopian king, had been killed in a quarrel over an ox, and it was common knowledge the argument had taken place simply because Hercules was itching for an excuse to fight. But one did not remind Hercules of things like that.

"Seen any natives here yet?" Hercules asked, hopefully. "Unfriendly?"

"Far from it. They met us very kindly with sheep and wine."

Already, through the darkness, they could see the friendly glow of the evening fire. By its light Jason could make out the figures of his companions busy at their tasks, fetching dry wood, collecting leaves for bedding, mixing wine and water for the feast that would follow the sacrifice to Apollo. A warm glow of contentment, like that of good wine, filled his heart.

"*Hercules!*"

The cry made Jason's scalp bristle, and he stopped dead as Hercules gripped his arm like an iron vise. It was a cry like an animal in agony, and it came, not from the camp, but from the brush to their far side.

"Who calls?" Hercules bellowed. "*Hylas!*"

"My lord!" A frantic figure came crashing through the brush, and Jason caught at it quickly or it would have fallen. It was not Hylas, but the lord Polyphemus, oldest among them, sinking down on his age-heavy limbs and gasping for breath. The old face he turned to Hercules was streaked unashamedly with tears.

"My lord, I was looking for you, when I heard a cry. Like a young lamb caught by a beast of prey. I alone was close enough to hear . . . I have searched, and searched. . . . Hercules, Hylas is gone. I checked the camp, and only he has not returned. Either robbers have got him, or the wild beasts. And there is no more cry."

Hercules was as a wild bull. The sweat poured down his forehead, his eyes glittered. The dark blood boiled, and with a cry of fury he flung down the pine and crashed off into the blackness.

Jason, and some of the others who had heard his cry, made as if to follow, but Polyphemus stopped them. "Let him go. It is too late now to be of use, but he needs to search. I will follow later in case he has need of someone. He loves that boy."

They waited, and there was silence, and then later, from far off in the blackness, a ringing, despairing cry. That was all. Back on the shore the Argonauts made their sacrifice, and had their meal, and presently laid themselves down to sleep, but they felt no joy.

As the morning star rose above the mountains, Jason felt a hand touch his shoulder. "The breeze has risen," Tiphys said. "Let's take advantage of it and sail at once, leaving this accursed place behind."

Quick in the pre-dawn darkness they broke camp, and boarded in eager haste. Willing hands pulled up the anchor stones and hauled in the ropes, and the sail belled out in the full wind. Soon *Argo* was far out to sea, passing Poseidon's Cape.

Slowly over the rim of the sea the bright dawn rose, gilding the ship's wake and the shoreline glistening with fresh dew. And from the *Argo* came a startled cry.

"Hercules!" "Hercules and Hylas. . . ." "Hercules is not here."

They stared, in the radiant dawn, at the empty midships seat.

"Nor Polyphemus either," a voice said quietly. "Hercules went to seek out Hylas, and Polyphemus followed Hercules."

The Minyae stared at each other as the enormity of their loss sank upon them. In their haste to be off before the wind, they had heedlessly left two of the best among them behind on the alien shore.

Fierce were the recriminations that arose, and tumultuous was the exchange of blame. But Jason took no part. He went away without a word and sat, paralyzed by utter helplessness. The storm broke above his head, yet he was as stone, his heart crushed utterly by the calamity.

Telamon stared at him, enraged. "Yes, sit there at your ease! This suits your purpose, doesn't it? Jason the great! You planned to abandon Hercules so his fame would not outshine your own!"

Still Jason sat, and Telamon swore a mighty oath. "Why do I waste my breath? We are going back, no matter how your accomplices try to stop me!" With that he made a rush at the helmsman Tiphys, his eyes blazing fire. As he sprang, so did Zetes and Calais, sons of the North Wind, spring to hold him back with main force and with stinging words. And the sea rose high, in the stiff and steady breeze, holding *Argo* in a mighty grip.

Then Mopsus the seer lifted his voice. "Do you not see? It is Nereus the sea-god who holds us. He is telling us that if we take Hercules with us to Colchis we defy the mighty Zeus. He belongs in Argos, where he has not yet accomplished his twelve labors. Nor must we weep for Polyphemus, for doubtless he is destined to meet a noble end in Mysia. As for Hylas for whom they went in search, no doubt a water nymph fell in love with him as he bent above the stream, and drew him under. But for us, we must sail on to Colchis with no turning back!"

So he cried, and the grey waters foamed high, dashing against the hollow ship, and then subsided into restless waves. The Argonauts, relieved, agreed that a god had spoken.

Telamon went straight to Jason where he sat, bowed beside the rail. He did not speak at first, but took Jason's hand in a firm grip, then embraced and kissed him. "Do not be angry. I spoke as a fool for I was blinded with distress. May the winds blow away the words and their offending, and may we, who have always been friends, be so again."

Jason gazed at the grey swirling sea and his wrath grew quiet. When he spoke, it was with wise forbearance. "You did indeed wound me when you accused me before all the others of having deliberately betrayed a loyal friend. But I do not mean to hold a grudge. You spoke not over worldly goods or property, but about a man, our comrade. I can only hope that if the need arises you will stand up for me as bravely as you did for him."

It was enough. Telamon and Jason sat down together, united as they had been before. All that day and that night *Argo* traveled under sail in a stiff wind. At daybreak the wind died, but Tiphys called that there was land ahead, and they saw a wide beach showing up from a bay. So they rowed the ship ashore as into the rising sun.

THE
BEBRYCES

AND WHAT," said Telamon happily, "do we have
here?"

The Argonauts were just beaching their ship and
clambering ashore on the dawn-gilded rocks when a welcoming party appeared atop the crest. That the welcome was
warlike was evident with one glance at the leader who, leaving
his compatriots behind, strode down to plant himself in the
Argonauts' midst. Jason, beholding him, called to mind some
monstrous offspring of old Mother Earth herself, for he was
knot-muscled, clad in a dark double mantle with ornate bronze
clasps and gripping a heavy staff of mountain olive. And the
sight was not displeasing. Jason felt his spleen rising and
realized that he was spoiling for a fight, that physical combat
was what he needed to drain off the pent-up tension of the
previous night. He saw the same thought mirrored in the
other's eyes.

Nor, obviously, was this alien reluctant to oblige. Not even
bothering to ask their names or mission, he spoke out bluntly.
"Hear me, you sailors! No stranger who puts in here can leave

64

without matching fists with mine. Pick your best man, and I
will fight him on the spot. Otherwise you will learn the con-
sequences to your sorrow."

This effrontery was all that was needed to kindle the Argonauts into a fury. I am the leader, Jason thought, so I should
call the challenge. But he was not sorry when the young Polydeuces rushed forward. Polydeuces the Spartan still bore upon
his cheeks the first down of youth, but he was reputed to be the
son of Zeus, and already his strength and spirit were equal to
that of a forest beast.

"Be still! Stranger, whoever you are, make no more show.
We accept your rules, and here I am to meet you of my own
free will."

His speech was as high-handed as the stranger's, and it was
met in kind. "Amycus, King of the Bebryces, stands ready to
teach you a lesson, *boy!*"

It would be, as Amycus had stated, a fight of one to one.
Jason felt his blood rising with expectation as the oddly assorted
pair, youth and man, threw off their cloaks and looked round
to settle upon a satisfactory patch of ground. In silence the
watchers on the cliff sat down, and the Argonauts did likewise
upon the sands. The two fighters paid no notice; they had eyes
only for each other, each taking the opponent's measure. Jason
was reminded of a wounded lion who, paying no heed to the
crowd that hems him in, concentrates only on the man who
injured him.

Polydeuces, having laid aside the loosely woven cloak that
had been a parting present from some Lemnian girl, began
making practice feints with both his arms. Amycus watched in
silence.

Idas nudged Jason's shoulder. "Look. He thirsts for blood,
that one." Jason nodded.

Now a servant placed at the feet of each a pair of ox-hide
gloves. "I make you a gift," Amycus said, "of whichever pair
you wish. Now bind them on. Later you can tell your compan-

ions of my skill at cutting rawhide and at drawing blood to the face of a man."

Polydeuces made no answer, only smiled quietly, and like the noble youth he was, drew on the pair that lay nearest to his feet. His brother Castor and the great Talaus stepped quickly forward to bind on the gloves and encourage him with a constant flow of low-voiced words. Likewise two of the strange watchers tended to the king, and while these preparations were completed the two warriors stood apart. At last all was ready. Their gloved fists high before their faces, the youth and the monstrous man moved toward each other with a will.

"Just so," Jason thought, "does a great wave rise up over a ship in a rough sea. And just at the moment overpowering seems inevitable, the lithe ship slips away, saved by a hair." So it was with Polydeuces. Although the king incessantly attacked, battering at him with nary a moment's rest, the slim youth had the skill to maneuver unscathed away from the heavy onslaught.

So it went for a time, until Jason saw that Polydeuces had taken the measure of his opponent's brutal style. Now his own style changed, and he stood up, returning blow for blow. Like the incessant din of a shipyard were the hammering strikes to cheek and jaw, and the dreadful sound of grinding teeth. There was no cessation until both were felled by their exhausted lungs, and as if by mutual consent they drew apart, shaking the sweat from their foreheads, eyeing each other and drawing great gasping breaths. Only a brief respite, then they were at it again, like two enraged bulls wrestling grimly for the same young mate.

Jason's own muscles ached in sympathy with Polydeuces as the youth twisted and dodged, parried and thrust again. Then he caught his breath, holding back an involuntary scream. Amycus had reared up to his full height, like a man striking down a sacrificial ox. Down came the heavy fist . . . Jason exhaled sharply as Polydeuces, warned by some instinct, jerked

his head away in a hairbreadth escape. The blow of Amycus'
forearm fell upon his shoulder. Polydeuces pivoted, closed in.
Like lightning his own blow descended, crashing above his
opponent's ear, smashing the skullbones in a death-rattle all
could hear.

Like a great beast, the fallen warrior sank to his knees in
agony and then fell still. It was over, and a shout of triumph
rang out from the Minyan lords.

"And now," Idas hissed at Jason's elbow, "for the rest of us!"
He picked up his ready axe, and Jason gripped his spear. Down
from the cliffs poured the Bebrycean horde, athirst with vengeance for their fallen king. With spears and clubs they charged
at the exhausted Polydeuces, but in a flash like lightning, the
Minyae were there before him, holding the attackers off the
young wrestler with their eager swords.

It was Polydeuces' brother Castor who drew first blood. As
an alien rushed towards him, he smote the man on the head
with such great force that the skull was split and the severed
halves fell from the shoulders to the right and left. Polydeuces
himself, spurred to a fury of recovery, made a running jump
at the next huge adversary, kicking him in the guts and laying
him in the dust. As the next came on he struck out with his
right hand, and there was a scream of pain. Jason gut retched;
Polydeuces' blow had torn off the alien's left eyelid, leaving the
eyeball bare.

A gasp and an oath came from Talaus as a spearthrust passed
beneath his belt, grazing the skin. A club blow fell on Iphitus,
knocking that staunch fighter to the ground where he lay
groaning but alive. Then the young Ancaeus wrapped his
great bearskin around his left arm as a shield, seized his huge
two-edged axe in his right hand, and flung himself into the
fray. Hard on his heels Telamon and Peleus hurled themselves.
Jason's heart pounded, and the blood rushed to his ears. He
gripped his spears.

"Hear, strangers! This is warlike Jason, son of Aeson!" With a fury he threw himself into the charge. It was at that moment, to his heart-secret satisfaction, that the line of the Bebryces broke.

"Like sheep thrown in panic on a winter's day when the grey wolves fall upon the fold," thought Jason in contempt. "We are like wolves, having only to inspect and choose our prey, while they wait helplessly and trample on each other." And he raised his voice in a clear triumphant cry.

"Hear, you world! This is the terror inspired by Jason and the Argonauts!"

Like a swarm of bees smoked from their hive the Bebryces fled. Far and wide they scattered, fleeing inland into their iron-bearing land, only to find that in their absence their vineyards and villages had been ravaged by a marauding tribe. On their heels came the victorious Minyae, rounding up with shouts of triumph whatever sheep and cattle the marauding band had left. With their prizes they fell back upon the beach and washed their bruises in the healing sea.

Through the heat of the day they rested on the shore, tending their wounded and tying their hawsers around a green bay tree. Then as the sun sank and the twilight fell, they prepared a mighty feast, and the fire of the immortal sacrifice blazed high. Castor tore down branches of the bay tree to crown his brother, shouting, "Hail, the mighty hero!" Telamon, too, to show his good feeling, made a wreath for Jason, and as the wine bowl was passed round they all did likewise, each crowning one another.

Orpheus took up his lyre, and in harmony with that celestial music they raised their voices in a song of praise of Polydeuces, the warrior son of Zeus. The wine went round, and in all that charmed night not one man closed his eyes.

Then came the dawn, and the chariot of the sun returned from the world's end to light the hillsides, spangled with morning dew. By its luminous rays the Minyae threw themselves laughing into the foam-tipped waves. They loosed the ropes that bound the *Argo* to the green bay tree and loaded aboard all booty of battle they thought might prove of use, then up the swirling Bosphorus they sailed before the morning wind.

The wind rose, sending the proud ship scudding in tempo with their spirits, and the sky greyed, yet such was their exhilaration that they did not care. They were the Minyae, conquerors of Amycus the Bebrycean, sailors of the seas of the known world. Those among them whose heads were lightest lifted their voices in spirited chantey with the pitching and the tossing of the waves.

Telamon grinned, lifting his face to the salt spray. "A good cure for too much blessing of Dionysian wine!"

Jason looked at a few of his noble companions, draped nonchalantly along the rail and smothered a grin. How fortunate that today they did not have to bend to the hard labor of the oars! Then from the prow came an appalling cry. The boat lurched, and Jason lifted his eyes and his heart jerked within him.

A great wave had arisen, like the hand of Poseidon, mountain-high. So high it seemed that it blotted out the clouds in the grey sky. No time to change direction or escape, no time for anything but to dive for shelter, to grip madly for handholds at the rail, and to pray, even those who did not believe in prayer. Afterwards, Jason was astonished at how swiftly the words of petition had arisen in his mind. The wave crested and broke, the spume rose, the *Argo* rode its height, and through it all Tiphys alone stood tall, his skilled hand firm upon the helm. At length the waves, like some dissatisfied sea monster, spewed the *Argo* forth into calmer waters. They were unhurt, though not one man among them but had come face to face with the black figure of his private fear. From that time on, those dark shadows were their fellow seamen.

They rested that night on the coast that faced the Bithynian shore.

They beached their ship, made it fast with ropes, and walked on shore; and there was no man whose legs did not shake beneath him, though pride forbade his betraying it in words. Jason himself made his way to a shale of rock and sat himself down, swept by a misery he was ashamed to speak. He was soaked with the salt spray, and the cold wetness had invaded even his leopard skin, making it no comfort against the inland breeze. That breeze was laden with a stench like rotten fish . . . around him he heard men retching, and his own stomach twisted.

"Jason? Jason! . . ."

His head jerked round at the thin painful cry.

From a rock dwelling he had not noticed, a grotesque figure staggered. A man so weak, so thin and old, it seemed obscene that he should be alive. His shriveled limbs trembled, his withered flesh was foully caked with dirt, his sightless eyes rolled in ceaseless searching as he groped his way by feel along the wall. Then the clawlike hands reached out in a blind seeking.

He was no one whom Jason had ever seen before. Yet as the helpless, bony fingers encountered Jason's shoulders, moved over the sea-wet leopard fur, and Jason did not flinch, a gift of recognition seemed to come. With a cry, the old figure fell to the earth in a prophetic swoon.

PHINEUS

THE MAN was Phineus. Phineus, once famous for his wealth and the gift of prophecy given him by Apollo. Phineus, son of Agenor, once king of Thrace. Strange was the tale he had to tell when he had recovered breath. Jason, beholding him, remembered his father Aeson, likewise brought low by age and suffering, and he was moved to weep.

When Phineus fell, the Argonauts had gathered in a circle round him, much amazed, and their amazement deepened when, his coma passing, he began to speak prophetic words.

"Hear me, you brave young men, pride and flower of all of the Hellenes. I know you, though I cannot see. You sail on *Argo*, led by Jason to seek the Golden Fleece at the command of a cruel king. Although Zeus has punished me with lingering old age and blinded eyes, knowledge of all things still comes to me through the gift of my lord Apollo, to whom I tender thanks despite the load of suffering that crushes me. I beseech you by our stern lord Zeus, god of the suppliants, by Phoebus Apollo, and by our lady Hera whose special favor I know has brought you here, that you save me, luckless and forsaken as

I am, from degradation and starvation. For I know by my oracle that none but you can do it."

"What evil afflicts you, old man? And what cruel fate brought it upon you?" Jason's voice was gentle.

The grotesque ghost of an ironic smile cracked the shriveled lips. "Not fate, but a god's gift. I am Phineus, blessed by Apollo with the gift of prophecy, and in my pride I used it to reveal to men the secrets of the gods. Including the sacred purposes of Zeus, and some not so sacred. For this Zeus the inscrutable has afflicted me with not only the curses you behold, but with another, which plagues me even more. Tell me, have you not already noticed something strange that burdens and pollutes our air?"

Jason nodded. Then, realizing the old man could not see, he answered aloud. "A stench of rot and death."

"You speak well. The stench rots what is wholesome, and will bring death to me, death that will come as a blessing, for in all this time no food has passed my lips. The people here take pity on my suffering; each day they bring me gifts of food, and each day, as I try to eat, vile feathered things, from the gods alone know where, swoop down from the sky and snatch it from my mouth. They come, and are gone, and there is no escape. What food they leave me stinks of putrefaction, for they befoul it all before they leave. So vile is the smell that no man dares come near."

Jason could well understand it. "You say that only we can help you? How?" he asked.

"I have been told by the oracle, and my own prophetic gifts, that these Harpies can be dealt with only by the sons of Boreas the North Wind, who were to sail with Jason. Nor need they fear assisting me, though you see by my suffering that the lord of the heavens is punishing a mortal man. Their compassion shall not cause them to lose favor with the gods. I swear by Apollo, giver of the prophetic gift, by my own ill-starred fortune and my blasted vision—by the dark Powers that dwell below the earth—that helping me will not bring down upon them wrath divine."

Thus spoke Phineus, and all who heard were moved to pity, but none more so than Zetes and Calais, the sons of the North Wind. They brushed their tears away, went up to the sad old man, and Zetes took his hand. There they swore to Phineus by all that they held sacred that they would drive away the Harpies when next they came. Indeed, if possible, they would slay them; their hands were already itching for their swords.

Immediately the youngest among them prepared for Phineus a goodly meal, and Zetes and Calais stationed themselves on either side, their sword arms ready.

Scarcely had Phineus raised to his trembling lips the first bite of food, when, like the crash of summer lightning, a raucous crying split the sky. Jason, despite himself, drew back in horror and instinctively threw his arm before his face. Down from the sky came— Birds? Beasts? More like beings in a loathsome trance-vision of the underworld. They were there, and the food was snatched from Phineus' lips so swiftly that the old man whimpered and a drop of blood rolled slowly down from the corner of his mouth. The area and the men were befouled with the creatures' filthy droppings. Then they were gone, as swiftly as they had come, leaving behind a stench so terrible that the men, wretching and gagging, were driven into the cleansing sea.

Yet, not all. The sons of the North Wind had flung their feathered guard-arms before their mouths and noses; their swords flashed, and like the Wind itself, they went flying in pursuit. Like a pair of keen hounds pressing close behind their quarry, they snapped at the feathers only just beyond their reach, and within moments pursued and pursuers were lost to sight.

Meanwhile the Argonauts, having washed themselves, bathed the filth from the old man's body and dressed him in his finest robes. Then they selected the choicest of the sheep they had just acquired at the expense of the deceased Amycus and made a splendid sacrifice and an even more splendid meal. They set out this fine banquet in the hall of Phineus, and sat down with him to enjoy it. Phineus ate ravenously; he was as joyous as a youth, as a man in a delightful dream.

All that night, for the second night, they ate and drank their fill and took no sleep, but waited awake for the return of the sons of the North Wind. And Phineus sat among them where the hearth-fire glowed, and told them all he dared of their future journey, to its very end.

"I cannot tell you all," he said. "Once I told all, to my folly. Now I realize the gods do not intend humanity to understand beforehand all of heaven's design.

"When you leave here, the first thing you will see is two great rocks, one on either side of a narrow strait. These are the Cycanian Rocks, through which, to my knowledge, no men have ever passed, for they have no firm foundation but frequently collide in a resounding roar and a seething mass of water, which brings only death. If you are sensible and take advice, do not rush in there rashly. Instead send out a dove. If she succeeds in flying between the Rocks and out to sea, then make haste to follow. But take a firm grip on the oars and cleave the water; your safety will depend not on prayers but on your strength of arms. Think of nothing else, concentrate thoughts and energies on the immediate task and do your praying earlier! If the dove flies but partway through and then comes to grief, turn back. The wise man always bows to the will of heaven. I implore you not to disregard this counsel from the gods."

Jason nodded, making mental note, and he saw Tiphys also looking alert and sober.

"What will come, will come," Phineus said, and there was a silence. "However, should you pass safely through, sail on. Shun the coastal waves of the Black Sea until you pass the mouth of the swift-flowing Rhebas and the Black Cape. There is harbor in the Isle of Thynias. Sail on, and beach on the coast of the Mariandyni on the opposite shore. From there a path leads down into the bowels of Hades; high above, from the very mountain top, the waters of dread Acheron gush up from the utter depths and torrent down to sea.

"Beyond are the hills of Paphlagonia, and further, opposite Helice the Bear, the lofty pinnacle of Carambis pierces the northern winds. Round this cape, and the whole of Aegialus will lie ahead. At its very end, where the coast juts into the sea, roar the rushing waters of the Halys and nearby, the River Iris foams out to sea. Next comes the River Thermodon, flowing into a quiet bay by the cape of Themiscyra, the plain of Doas."

Jason hoped devoutly that Tiphys was committing all of this to mind. His own brain whirled. Phineus' old voice poured on relentlessly.

"Nearby lie the three towns of the Amazons. Next the Chalcybes, to whom no morning brings a holiday; they work the reluctant ground for the iron it yields. Near them are the sheep-raising Tibareni, and the forest-dwelling Mossynoeci, who live in wooden towers. When all these lie behind, beach your ship on the low-lying island you will find. But first you must find a way of driving off the Stymphalian birds."

These latter words sent a shudder of recognition up Jason's spine, and he saw two or three of his companions exchange uneasy glances. The great birds were notorious for the violence that revealed them sacred to Mars, and even Hercules with his might and his unerring aim had been unable to destroy them. Why beach there? The question formed in Jason's mind, but Phineus the soothsayer gave answer before he could frame it into words.

"Wait there, I advise you, for a little while. Out of the bitter brine will come a godsend."

"What?" Jason cried eagerly.

Phineus shook his head. "Not again will I sin against the gods by telling all I see. Wait, and you will learn. But I tell you this. Beyond this isle of Mars dwell many tribes—the Philyres, the Macrones, the Becheiri, the Sapeires, the Byzeres. Then you will come to the beginnings of the land of Colchis. Still sail on, until you come to the farthest corner of the Black Sea, the end of the world itself. There a broad river rolls swiftly down to sea and there, in the dark grove of Ares, you will find the Golden Fleece. It is spread on the topmost branches of a sacred oak, guarded by a great serpent who does not sleep."

He ceased. In the long silence there was no sound except the crackling of the fire. At length Jason spoke for them all, and his voice was filled with his misgivings.

"My lord, you have told us all the dangers of our voyage until the moment that we reach our destination. You have told us the secret of the Clashing Rocks. For this, I assure you, you have the gratitude of all. But there is a greater question that I know beats in the breast of each man here. Shall we and *Argo* ever see again the shores of home? My heart sinks within me, I know not how to manage, nor how I am to find my way again across the uncharted seas. My companions are as inexperienced as myself, and we all know that Colchian Sea lies at the far end of the world."

"Son," said old Phineus gently, and his eyes were kind, "seek to know no more, for it is not good for men to pierce too deeply into the unknown. Yet will I tell you this. If you escape the hateful Rocks, you need fear no more. Some Power will guide you back to Hellas by a different way. And remember this. In all your venture you can find no better ally than Aphrodite with her subtle arts."

Jason stared at him blankly. Of all the Olympians, certainly that fickle lady was the last to which an adventurous man would show devotion.

Before he could speak, there came a rush of wind, as the beating of mighty wings, and when they all turned, the sons of Boreas stood behind Jason, just burst in through the night-shut door. Gasping for breath and thoroughly pleased with their exertions, Calais and his brother collapsed onto the cushions and accepted the wine bowls offered by their eager friends.

"The monsters took refuge in a great cavern under the cliffs of Dicte!" Zetes poured out the tale, with emphasis on the length and ardor of the chase.

"They are not dead then!"

Zetes shook his head. "We almost had them. But Iris of the rainbow, messenger of the gods, leaped down from the sky, reminding us that the Harpies are, after all, the hounds of Zeus. But you need not fear. They will not trouble Phineus again. The rainbow was Zeus' oath by the sacred River Styx, that oath which not even the greatest of the gods may break."

All were delighted with the news, and Jason turned to Phineus, embracing him, his heart overflowing with real kindness.

"There is a god then, after all," he said. "One who cares for you and who has brought us here from alien lands that the sons of Boreas could save you. Only one thing remains for my full happiness, that I might see you now restored to sight."

Sadly the old man shook his head. "My eyes are ruined beyond recall. I pray instead for the coming of sweet death, for with her soft blessing I shall enter into rest and peace."

So for a little, like father and son, the two men talked, until slowly, over the threshold of the open door, the first rays of dawn crept. With their coming, the Argonauts beheld a strange procession making its silent way from inland to Phineus' rocky shore. A smile lit the old man's face as he perceived the footsteps.

"My friends, my people." Old and young were there, and each bore an offering from a home's supply—a covered dish, a bunch of grapes, a bowl of wine. These were they who for years had daily, vainly, attended to the old man's needs. Today they found him nourished and rested, surrounded by golden strangers and his afflictors gone. And great was their rejoicing and their praise of the Minyan lords.

With sage replies the aged Phineus satisfied his kindly vis-

itors and dismissed them, all save one. This was Paraebius, his
closest friend, to whom he had long before confided his hopes
of rescue by the sons of Boreas. He made Paraebius acquainted
with his noble guests, then bid him go and fetch the finest of
his flocks. When Paraebius had gone, Phineus turned to the
Argonauts and smiled.

"You see there proof that not all men are forgetful of help
that has been given. Once that man knew no rest from labor;
the harder he toiled, the harder he found his life, and daily he
sank lower. He was suffering for a sin committed by his father,
who in the arrogance of his youth had despoiled an age-old
forest oak. I advised him how to make atonement for his father's sin, and he escaped the wrath of heaven. Never since that
day has he neglected me. He is so determined to stand by me
that I can hardly even get him to leave my house!"

With these very words Paraebius reappeared, leading two
sheep without flaw or blemish. These, at eventide, Jason and
the sons of Boreas sacrificed at Phineus' command. They worshipped Apollo, lord of prophecy, around the hearth of Phineus
the prophet, and the younger men, as was the custom, prepared
a splendid feast. When all had enjoyed it, they laid themselves
down to sleep. It was the first time in three nights that they
had done so.

THE SHORES OF THE
MARIANDYNI

T HEY HAD PLANNED to sail at dawn, but in that grey hour there swept down the Etesian Winds, blowing fiercely. For forty days, as Zeus had long before ordained, those winds refreshed the Minoan Islands, scorched by the Dog Star, Sirius. For forty days, the Argonauts waited restlessly in the land of Thynia; and every day, knowing it would please their lord Phineus, the people sent gifts for the sustaining of the golden strangers. Then the winds died, and in the first calm dawn the young lords raised an altar on the beach to the Olympian gods, the blessed twelve. Upon it they laid choice offerings, and then they girded themselves and waded through the morning sea to board proud *Argo*. Eagerly they sat down at the oars. And Euphemus sheltered in his great hands a shy dove, who huddled in her feathers, trembling with fright.

As they rowed diligently through the cool misty morning, a single cloud swept down from the distant skies and seemed to follow, hovering above the mast; Euphemus looked up, squinting against the spray.

"Athene, the grey-eyed goddess, watches over us." And the men took heart and put fresh speed into their rowing.

Soon they were entering the narrowest passage of the winding strait. On either side high crags loomed to hold the waters in, and *Argo* vibrated with the swirling current. Fear began to possess the hearts of the Minyan lords. The surf rose high, and ceaselessly its thunder pounded in their ears.

"Not far now. The rocks grow closer." Euphemus stood up, thrusting the terrified dove inside his cloak, and made his way up to the prow where he stood like a fierce statue pushing through the spray.

"All strength! *Row!*" Tiphys' command rang out. *Argo* shot forward as if the men sought by their own vain strength to drive her through the rocks. As a crash rang near ahead, *Argo* swept round a bend. And over all the shipmates a silence fell.

They were beholding a sight which no one else would ever see. Slowly, inexorably, the great cliffs were moving apart. The hearts of the Argonauts were heavy with premonitions they dared not speak. Then Euphemus, with one swift gesture, flung his cloak open. In a flash of white the young dove fluttered and was gone, winging through the passage, and the eyes of all were upon her in her flight. Already, as she flew, the Rocks approached each other. She looks so small against them, Jason thought irrelevantly. Valiantly her wings battled past the ever-nearing cliffs.

Crash! The sea roared, and the wide skies rang, and *Argo* shuddered in every seam and joining. The men, flung off balance, were blinded as the foam swept high. Below them, in the very bowels of the earth, subterranean caverns bellowed out like souls in torment as the sea surged in. Round and round *Argo* spun like a helpless top. Jason, cowering unashamedly behind the shelter of his leopard skin, remembered the old tales Chiron had told of the creation of the earth from Chaos, and for the first time his conscious mind believed.

Through the tumult and the swirling spray a voice penetrated. A voice, eager and excited. Euphemus' voice. "Look! Look!"

The Rocks were opening, and as they did a small flutter of feathers, like the dusting of first snow, fell gently from them. Far ahead, in open sunlight, they beheld a small white form flying free.

"She lost the tips of her tail feathers," Euphemus said, "but she's flying! She got through!"

And from all the length and breadth of *Argo* came a cry of triumph, and the proud ship herself joined with them in the shout of joy.

"*Row!*" Tiphys shouted against the din. "Quick, while the rocks are open!" Instantly they put their full strength into it, with no time to think and grateful for it, for their hearts despite the dove were full of dread. Their backwash surged and overtook them, thrusting *Argo* ever more swiftly into the narrow pass, and then, irrevocably, there was no turning back. The Rocks were closing, and panic drowned out fear. Jason closed his eyes and threw himself doggedly into the all-demanding task of controlling the heavy oar.

"Almost! I can see open sea!" he heard someone shout, and then there was a gasp of terror, and even the god-fearing men gave voice to involuntary oaths. Before them, like a third cliff raised by the hand of an angry Titan, loomed a wall of water, breaking into a crash of foam to fall upon them. They bent their heads in fear and dread, all except Tiphys who alone stood firm, a solitary figure upon the deck, pulling fiercely at the steering rod as *Argo,* like a frightened mare, plunged and rose. The ship swerved, and the great wave slid safely underneath her keel.

The wave slid, and rose, lifting *Argo* high and propelling her back towards the Clashing Rocks.

"*Row!*" Euphemus yelled. With answering shouts, his comrades put their whole backs into it. The oars bent like curved bows against the water's terrible force, but for every foot *Argo* gained, she was carried back two, back into the Clashing Rocks.

Another wave rose high and rushed down upon them. *Argo* shot like a rolling pin into a hollow of the sea, and was held by the tide at the very point where the Rocks would meet. To left and right the sheer terrible walls closed in with a primordial rumble, and the exhausted sailors' arms were near to breaking, but *Argo* would not budge.

Suddenly the wind seemed to change. The cloud that had hovered over them moved downward and became one with the mist behind them, and the currents shifted. With a sudden thrust, as if some hand of the gods propelled it, the gallant ship clove the air like a proud-winged arrow and was clear, just as the Rocks clashed with a roar behind her. *Argo* shuddered and moaned, and the tip of her mascot was sheared off by the cliffs as they came together.

They were through, and otherwise unscathed. Slowly, and trembling unashamedly, the men lifted their faces to the sun-bright sky. Ahead of them the ocean stretched, vast and serene.

They felt like men who had emerged from Hell.

It was some time before they could trust themselves to speak. "I think," Tiphys said at last, carefully, "it is safe to say that all is well. For *Argo,* and for us. Euphemus was right; Athene herself was with us in the cloud. We have escaped a certain death. How can we but believe there is some law in heaven that protects our ship?"

Still Jason sat, and Tiphys came to stand over him, his voice tinged with impatience. "So now, my lord, since the gods themselves brought us safely through the Clashing Rocks, I beseech you to stop dreading so the duty assigned you by your king. Did not Phineus tell you there are no further obstacles you need to fear?"

With that Tiphys strode back to the helm and commenced to steer straight across the sun-sparkled sea. And the others, who had heard his words, concentrated on their rowing, deeming it unwise to interfere.

Jason, too, bent across his oar. He was grateful for the physical activity, for his mind was teeming with self-questions. His anger, which had quickly risen, as quickly died.

Tiphys was right. What more was there to fear? They had come safely through what seemed the mouth of hell itself . . . through the advice of Phineus and the skill of Tiphys. No thanks to Jason. *No,* Jason thought with sudden revulsion, Jason the golden had cowered like a spineless child and given way to traitorous despair. Jason, son of Aeson! Would the others accept him as leader anymore?

His mind raced, searching out the right move. At last, swallowing his pride, he went to Tiphys and made a gentle answer.

"Tiphys, I appreciate your kind intentions, your trying to give me comfort in my torment. But in my blindness I have made a fatal error. When Pelias commanded me to make this quest, I ought to have refused at once though my life be forfeit. Instead I accepted eagerly, seeking glory and honor, and ever since my days and nights have been obsessed with intolerable fears. Not for myself; for you."

Jason's voice, though quiet, carried well. He knew, without taking his eyes from Tiphys, that he had their full attention.

"Yes, I shrink from the thought of the cruel sea we cross, and of what will happen when we land and find the natives hostile, as they will surely be. And why? Because of the danger to you all, my friends, who so courageously have rallied to my side. It is easy for you to be cheerful, Tiphys. You have only your own life to worry about. But I am concerned, not with myself, but with each and all of you. How can I be sure that I will bring you safely again to home?"

He waited a split second, fairly holding his breath. Then he knew with relief that all was well, the crisis past. His words were accepted with cries of acclamation and reassurance, and he turned to the others freely, flashing a boyish grin.

"What need I fear with friends like you behind me? Your courage kindles mine and fills me with confidence to face whatever comes. But now that we have passed safely through the Clashing Rocks, I have no reason to expect any further danger, so long as we follow the route that Phineus held before us."

The discussion was closed. Jason returned to his seat, and for the rest of the day he and all the others put all their energies into their rowing.

The River Rhebas . . . a mountain peak . . . the Black Cape; the mouth of the River Phyllis and then broad plains . . . All day and all the windless night the Minyae labored, ploughing the salty ocean with their oars. At last, as utter darkness began giving way to the first faint gleam of light, they put to harbor at Thynias' lonely isle, and waded ashore near unconscious with exhaustion.

As they reached the beach, they turned back towards the sea just as the dawn broke through. A breeze like a faint gasp moved among them, and they grew still as statues. Through the clouds, slanting like golden arrows, came the rays of sun, and in them, moving north, to their dazzled eyes . . .

"The lord Apollo," Orpheus breathed.

The rays, the wisps of clouds took on the shape of vision . . . the golden locks, the silver bow and quiver . . . the island quaked and the sea ran high, and the Minyae, awestruck, bowed their heads and dared not lift their eyes.

The clouds dissolved, the chariot of the sun rose high, and it was over. "Come," Orpheus said at last. "We will dedicate this island to Apollo of the Dawn. Here where we stand we will build an altar on the shore and offer to him libations and the scent of offerings, and later, if he grants us safe return to Thessaly, we will sacrifice to him the horned goats of our homeland."

At once they began the work. Some built an altar, others scattered in search of a fawn or a wild goat. When they had found their quarry, with all ritual they wrapped the thighbones in fat and burned them on the sacred altar and in a wide circle they danced around the blazing sacrifice.

Glory to Phoebus,
Glory to the Healing God!

Orpheus took his lyre and sang to them of Apollo, how long ago in his glorious youth he had slain the monster Delphyne beneath Parnassus' rocky brow, and how the nymphs had encouraged the youthful god with the very song they sang him now.

After they had worshipped Apollo with dance and song, they made holy libations. And then, touching the sacrifice as they swore, they took a sacred oath: *"We will stand by one another in unity forever."*

With the third day's dawning, a fresh wind rose and again they put to sea. Soon all the landmarks Phineus had promised approached, passed, and lay behind. The mainland coast, the fertile lands and rivers. . . . All day the halyards quivered in the wind. During the night the breeze dropped, and with the dawn they gratefully made harbor by the lofty cliffs of the Cape of Acherusias. Here, near the windy Cave of Hades and the sheer waterfall of Acheron, they prepared to camp on the land of the Mariandyni.

Almost at once the natives of the place appeared, and at their head a stalwart figure—Lycus, king and chieftain. With open arms and offers of alliance he hailed the Argonauts as slayers of the insolent Amycus. As for Polydeuces, who had struck the fatal blow, the people flocked to him from all sides as to a god, for long had the insolent Bebryceans terrorized their shores. There was no seaside camp for the Argonauts that day, but wine and feasting and convivial conversation in the palace. And Jason recounted for the noble king the name and lineage of each of his companions, and all the adventures that had befallen them.

Lycus was fascinated, but when Jason spoke of the abandoned Hercules, the king's face sobered.

"What a powerful ally to have lost from your hard journey!

Well I remember seeing him at my brother's funeral games; Hercules beat our own greatest boxer and knocked out all his teeth. After that he subdued all four of the neighboring tribes who used to prey upon our lands. Since that day none have dared rise against us save the brutal Bebryceans, and now they have suffered for their insolence through you. I thank the gods that the son of Tyndareus killed Amycus and thus provoked the Bebryceans to a losing battle. To recompense you, I shall send my own son, Dascylus, with you on your journey. His presence among you will assure you of friendly encounters all along your way. And more, I will build, high on the Acherusian Cape, a temple to the son of Tyndareus, which will be seen and honored by sailors far at sea."

All day and through the night they sang and feasted, and the wine poured freely, and the youthful Dascylus joined them, eager for the glorious adventure that his father had promised. As the first light streaked the sky, they left the palace, hurrying and laughing; for they were mellow with the blessing of Dionysus. And Lycus himself went with them, loading them down with gifts too great to number.

Jason, running haphazardly through the fresh grey wind of dawn, felt his heart lifting. It would have been wiser, perhaps, to have drunk less wine. But wine was a great builder of the spirits. There was not much further to make journey, Lycus had said. And had not Phineus promised them safe passage?

"*A-a-a-aghh!*" The cry split the still morning, sobering them sharply. Jason swerved left, towards the muddy river from whence the sound had come, but Idas, thrashing through the reeds, passed him and was the first to reach the river shore. Jason, dashing up a moment later, found Idmon doubled up among the reeds, blood gushing from his thigh.

"Boar," he gasped. "Must have been lying in the river . . . gored me. . . ."

Idas bent over him. "The bone is broken."

"Look out!" Jason shouted. The evil beast had leapt out of its hiding place and now charged again. Swiftly Peleus flung his javelin, but it missed its mark. It was Idas' well-aimed spear that struck the monster, and it fell, impaled, with a loud grunt. They left the beast there in his death agony and with sorrowing hearts carried their wounded companion back to the ship for tending. But it was no use; as soon as they were safe aboard the *Argo,* Idmon died in his comrades' arms.

There was no further thought of sailing on. For three days the Minyae mourned their friend, and the Mariandyni and their king, Lycus, sorrowed with them. On the fourth day they rose early and robed themselves in mourning and went ashore. Jason walked among them, ordering the funeral rites, but one among their number was counted missing. Tiphys, who had been taken ill, remained aboard to rest at his comrades' earnest wish.

Down to the shore came the men of the Mariandyni, led by Lycus the king, and together they and the Minyae laid Idmon in the earth, Idmon the soothsayer who had foreseen his own death far from home, but who nonetheless had come to sail on *Argo.* Many sheep were slaughtered in his honor, and a barrow raised, the trunk of a wild olive, which might still be seen, alive and putting forth fresh leaves in the latter days. The funeral games were celebrated, and only then did the Minyae, with Dascylus among them, return to death-still *Argo.*

Returned, and wept, and were as figures cut in stone. For there on *Argo* they found another comrade fallen. Tiphys lay as if asleep, but life had left him while his comrades were paying funeral honors to Idmon, son of Abas.

None could explain the cause of this new death, and none could measure the depth of grief and despair to which it plunged them. Again they went through the motions of funeral ritual, laying Tiphys in the earth beside Idmon, and then cast themselves down silently by the shore of the quiet sea. Despair wrapped around them; all hope was gone, all spirit left.

It was Ancaeus at last who rose, Ancaeus, who had been

reared beside the sea. To Peleus he went, for he dared not speak to Jason in his present mood.

"There is no sense in wasting our time in this godforsaken place. And no sense in giving up the quest. Has Jason forgotten why he brought me with him? Because I am a fighter? No! Because I am a steersman, and know ships. And not I alone, but others here as well. You need have no fears for *Argo*. I beg you, remind the others boldly of their duty."

Peleus took the measure of Ancaeus and was satisfied. Quickly he told the others of his thinking.

"To mourn our fallen comrades is right and proper, but too much grief is unprofitable and unmanly. Two men have died; the destiny of us all is in the hands of the gods. We must not fight it, but we must not give in. We have other steersmen here; we must sail on. Awake and work, and throw sorrow to the winds."

"Where are these pilots?" Jason asked bitterly. "Tiphys was best among us, and we all knew it. The other skilled seamen on whom we all relied are even more unmanned than I. What is the use? The fate that awaits us is as sad as that of our lost friends. We can neither reach Colchis nor find our way back to home. We are doomed to grow old and die here, in this foreign land."

No fame. No glory. Nothing done. It was to Jason the most terrible fate of all.

THE BEACH
AT COLCHIS

NONETHELESS, on the twelfth day *Argo* again took to the sea. At dawn they boarded, rowed out from the mouth of Acheron, and shook the broad sail out in the morning wind. Ancaeus was at the helm, by vote of his companions who chose him over Erginus, Nauplius and Euphemus, all able and eager. And Jason sat in his accustomed place and cursed himself for his lack of faith and skill.

The sail belled in the breeze beneath clear skies. Past the mouth of the River Callichorus, sacred to the dance of Dionysus, they sailed, and past a shore where rose a barrow tomb. Here a light, flashing on the rocks, caused the Argonauts to turn and observe a warlike figure. It rose on the edge of the tomb and gazed out to sea in splendid panoply of purple-crested helmet and bronze armor; then, as they passed by, sank from sight.

"It is the ghost of Sthenelus, son of Actor, who died fighting with Hercules against the Amazons," declared Mopsus the seer. And he bade them land and lay the ghost with libations and holy sacrifice. And so they did, giving honor to the tomb of

Sthenelus and sacrificing sheep. In a separate place they raised an altar to Apollo, Saver of Ships, and burned the thighbones of the sheep. And Orpheus also dedicated there a lyre.

The wind still blew, so again they went aboard and let out the sail. Eagerly over the sea *Argo* flew, like a high hawk gliding across a sunstruck sky. Past gentle Parthenius, past Sesamus and the peaks of Erythini and Crobialus, Cromna, and Cytorus, on through the night. At sunrise Cape Carambis lay at hand. The wind ceased; all day and all that night they rowed along the endless shores. At last they landed on the Assyrian coast where Deileon, Phlogius and Autolycus greeted them. These men, companions once of Hercules, had been living in that place since being separated from that brawny hero. On seeing the Argonauts and marking their rank, the three at once came forward, introduced themselves and expressed a fervent desire to leave for good. With hearty spirits Jason welcomed them aboard, and they at once embarked, for the northwest wind offered a release from rowing. That same day *Argo* rounded the distant headland of the Amazons. In the bay beyond, encountering rough seas, Ancaeus ran the ship ashore.

Here was the mouth of the Thermodon, river unique, divided like none other into a multiplicity of branches. The parent river, flowing down from the Amazonian Heights, burst in an arch of cresting foam into the sea.

The Unfriendly Sea, thought Jason. It was well named. And on its farther shore lay their elusive goal, Colchis, so near and yet so far. Colchis, Phrixus' alien adopted home.

Jason was not displeased when a fair wind rose, enabling them to again set out to sea before an encounter with the Amazons, although there were some groans aboard over missing the opportunity for contact with those warlike women. Time enough for such battles and other interchanges after we have won the fleece, Jason thought. Irrelevantly he wondered what the women of the Colchians would be like. The thought passed quickly; his mind was intent on the glory of his quest and like most Greeks his taste did not run to foreign women.

By night they reached the black bleak land of the iron-mining Chalcybes, who lived a life of endless toil, and next the country of the Tibareni, of the strange childbirth customs, where the husband took to his bed and groaned in travail to mislead evil spirits away from his laboring wife. Then came the Sacred Mountain and the high ground of the Mossynoeci of the wooden homes. Ribald laughter swept up and down *Argo*'s deck as those much-traveled or given to bawdy tales shared the rumors they had heard. "What we do in public, the Mossynoeci do at home, and they do openly in the marketplace those things a civilized Greek would do only in the privacy of his own room!"

"There's much truth in the saying all foreigners are barbarians."

During that night the faint wind died, and with the dawn a day of hard rowing lay before them. In late afternoon a great bird circled above them in the air. Suddenly it dove, skimming directly above their startled heads. A great plume plummeted from a flapping wing, and pierced noble Oileus' shoulder. In his shock, he let his oar slip from his grasp. At once his seatmate, Eribotes, plucked out the feather and bound the wound with the leather band of his own scabbard.

"Look out!" a second bird swooped down, but this time Clytius had his arrow ready. The bird fell, spilling into the water beside the ship.

Now Amphidamas was moved to speech. "These birds must mean we are close to the Isle of Ares. Why Phineus told us to land here, the gods alone yet know; but if we mean to do so, we must devise a plan. Hercules once drove off the Stymphalian birds with the din of a bronze rattle. Let us put on our crested helmets to protect our heads, then half of us shall row while the others protect the ship with spears and shields. If we all shout and yell, we may frighten the accursed birds away with the screeching and the waving plumes and upraised spears. When we land, we can make further din by banging on our shields."

The suggestion pleased them all. Their bronze armor soon glinted, and their purple crests waved above their heads. They locked their shields together, a kind of roof above the ship, and from below arose a roar like the meeting of opposing armies on the battlefield. But no other bird did they see until they beached on the island and banged their shields. Then as the clamor reverberated through the marshes, birds by the thousands rose in panic in the air. A rain of feathers fell, blotting out the falling sun, as the bird army fled for the mainland hills. But beneath their shields the Argonauts sat like comfortable townspeople hearing hailstones on the roof.

The light died with dusk, and the North Wind fell upon the sea with fearsome force. The billows rose with a shrieking blast, and a dark mist blotted out the sky, and no star shone. The Argonauts, secure in their beached ship, gave thanks, and thought gratefully of Phineus.

All through the night, rain fell in torrents, and the sea screamed, but as the murky darkness gave way to misty grey, the rainfloods ceased. The world was still and chill, veiled in clouds of fog. In its impalpable softness everything seemed to shimmer in a soundless waiting. And the promise of Phineus hammered in Jason's brain: *"Out of the bitter brine will a god-send come."*

Ancaeus of the sailor's farseeing eyes approached. "We have been blessed. During the storm another ship was wrecked. I have seen the pieces of a splintered hull float by."

Jason came to a rapid decision. "Let us form a searching party. If there are survivors, it may be they can advise us on the route we have yet to go." A faint tentative sun was now beginning to sift through the thick-hanging mist. Quickly an exploring party was prepared, and Jason himself went with them, pulling his leopard skin close around his shoulders.

It was Jason who saw them first. Four men, young as themselves and as noble in their bearing, though so exhausted and battered by the elements that they were less alive than dead. Yet when they beheld the Minyae they straightened and came forward fearlessly with their weary heads held high, and Jason knew the measure of their worth.

The eldest among the strangers was the first to speak. "Whoever you are, we call on you by Zeus the All-Seeing to aid us in our need. We are brothers, sailing on a family mission, but our rotten craft has been shattered by a gale at sea. We beg you, as you are like to us in age and, by the look of you, equals in rank, to take pity on us. Give us clothes and look after us, for the sake of Zeus who is the strangers' god."

Again the words of the prophecy rang in Jason's ears, and he responded to the young man with cautious questions. "We shall be glad to give you all you need. But tell me first, who are you? What is your rank? From whence come you, and what business makes you dare these dangerous seas?"

The stranger's arm had gone to his head, as if he were half-dazed by all he had endured, but at Jason's challenge his eyes narrowed with fierce pride. "From wherever you come, you must have heard of Phrixus of the Golden Fleece, who came to Colchis a fugitive from Hellas. This foreign prince was welcomed by King Aetes who married him to his daughter Chalciope. These two became our parents. Phrixus is dead, and we carry out his dying wish by sailing to Orchomenus to claim the estate of our grandfather Athamas. This is my brother Cytissorus; this, Phrontis; this, Melas. As for me, I am Argus, son of Phrixus the prince!"

At these words, the Argonauts present were overcome with awe and joy. Jason himself held out both his arms, and his voice rang in exultation. "It must have been some god who brought you to me! We are kinsmen, Argus. My grandfather Cretheus was brother to Athamas, and I, like Phrixus, travel from Hellas to the land of Colchis. I am Jason, son of Aeson the lawful king!"

And they embraced, and each felt a kinship of pride as well as blood.

First the immediate needs were tended. Willingly the Argonauts shared their own clothing with their new companions. Then all of them made their way together to the Temple of Ares built in a bygone hour by the Amazons. There, at the small stone roofless structure, they sacrificed sheep, burned them on the altar, prepared a feast, and ate.

At last Jason rose to address the sons of Phrixus. He surveyed them shrewdly, summoning all his eloquence. Surely this was the godsend Phineus promised, but how could he best win Argus to his cause? Argus, he knew instinctively, was no easily dazzled fool.

"Truly," he began, "Zeus is the all-seeing god. All we who fear the gods and uphold the right will at one time or another catch his eye. See how he rescued Phrixus from the trap of the murderous Ino and moreover heaped upon him riches and honor. See how now he has brought you unscathed through the dreadful storm. Now you have opportunity to board our ship, which is under the protection of Athene the wise, and to journey west or east, whichever you desire. Will you not in turn help me, guiding us to Colchis and aiding us in bringing away the Golden Fleece that I may return it to its rightful place in Hellas? This is my mission, to atone thereby for the intended sacrifice of Phrixus."

Jason spoke with a golden tongue, but his words were greeted by a silence. He saw Argus and his brother exchange shocked glances. At last Argus himself rose to make reply.

"Our friends and kinsmen . . . we pledge ourselves to help you to the best of our ability in times of trouble. But I confess the thought of sailing with you now fills my heart with dread. My grandfather Aetes can be a deadly enemy. He calls himself the son of Helios, but his voice and build could be the envy of the god of war himself. It will be no easy task to take the fleece without the permission he will never give. Night and day it is guarded by a serpent who cannot die and who never sleeps, an immortal offspring of old Earth herself."

The faces of many of the listeners grew pale, and Jason's with them. But soon Peleus replied with spirit.

"You need have no such fears. We are, after all, not unused nor unskilled in fighting. We know as much of war as the king of Colchis, and are equally related to the happy gods. If Aetes does not freely give us the fleece of gold, his warlike tribesmen will be of little use to him, you may be sure!"

Peleus and Argus continued the debate until, satisfied with their supper, they all retired to rest. With the dawn they raised the sail to a gentle breeze and left the Isle of Ares, the sons of Phrixus with them.

By nightfall they passed the Isle of Philyra where Chiron the beloved centaur had been conceived. Past the lands of the Macrones and the far-ranging Becheiri, *Argo* sailed, past the territories of the Sapeires and the Byzeres with a light wind billowing her gallant sail. Late the next afternoon, the last reaches of the Black Sea opened fair before them, and they beheld with awe the Caucasus' mighty peaks, and afar off the ever-circling eagle. The wind brought to them the brave Prometheus' shrieks of pain from the high mountaintop, where he was forever chained for defying the gods to bring the gift of fire to man.

Night fell, wrapping *Argo* in her impenetrable cloak; but with Argus to guide them, Ancaeus steered her true into the broad estuary of the Phasis River at the farthest reach of the Unfriendly Sea. Quickly they lowered the sail and the very mast itself; then they rowed straight into the mighty river, which rolled with foam. To the left lay the peaks of Caucasus and Aea, city of Aetes, to the right the Plain of Ares and the war-god's sacred grove.

Jason peered vainly towards it through the pitch-dark night. Somewhere there in the darkness, guarded by its never-sleeping serpent, glowed the Golden Fleece spread on the branches of a holy oak.

Turning, he took from his belongings a golden cup, with his

own hands filled it with an offering of honey-sweet wine, and poured it into the river's foam. He called on Earth herself, and the gods of this foreign land, and the spirits of its famous sons, to give him help, friendship and happy harbor.

"We have reached the land of Colchis." Ancaeus' voice was quiet at Jason's shoulder. "Now we must consider whether to speak to Aetes honestly, or to take what we seek by stealth or force."

"Jason." Argus, prince of Colchis, had come up behind them so silently that they both jumped, exchanging uneasy glances. Argus ignored Ancaeus, addressing himself directly to his own kinsman. "Order your men to row in among the reeds and anchor your ship where she cannot be seen."

Jason did as Argus had advised, and they moored the ship with stone. There they sat, and all the rest of that dark night they waited, eager and expectant, for the dawn.

ARRIVAL AT
THE PALACE

DAWN CAME to the young lords, lying concealed among the water rushes. It came shrouded in soft mist, rolling like the smoke of sacrifice in from the sea. Jason, who had risen with the first faint light, lifted his face to it, felt the soft damp of it against his face, and laughed aloud.

"A gift of Hera! What have we to fear?"

Only stillness answered, and he curbed his bright confidence and turned in silence to face the others. Each had taken his own seat on the *Argo*'s benches, and it seemed to Jason, watching, that this hidden marshy hollow had become a conference hall. The reeds were their walls, the masts their pillars, the grey mist closing ever closer a concealing roof. He looked at the row on row of quiet listeners who sat waiting. His friends. Some had been playmates of childhood, companions of youth, sharers of the horseplay and wild bragging. All, bonded by what they had shared in this quest for high adventure, had found friendships that only death could break. Some, death had claimed already. His wild elation of the earlier moment had passed, and when he spoke, it was quietly and with his heart.

97

"Friends." He looked at each in turn. How the quest had tempered and hardened them, turning them from youths to men. "I will tell you what I would choose to do. But its success will depend on you. We share the danger, so we share the right of speech. I warn you, if you keep your mouths shut now instead of speaking your minds, you could jeopardize our success. So hear me out, but then for the gods' sake tell me what you think."

He paused. Yes; he had them all. He took a deep breath. "I ask you all to stay here quietly while I go to the palace."

There was a stir of reaction, quickly suppressed. "I will take with me the sons of Phrixus and two others. I want to parley with Aetes, give him a chance to treat us as friends and offer freely the Golden Fleece. If he dismisses us contemptuously, relying on his strength, we will know what to think. Then we can decide whether to fight or to find some way of getting what we seek without resort to violence. It is wrong to use force to rob him of his own, if words might win him over. Speech often smooths the way where force has failed."

They had learned the truth of that, Jason thought, during this voyage. He saw some heads nodding in remembrance, and pressed his advantage. "Aetes welcomed my kinsman Phrixus when he fled from a stepmother's treachery and a father's knife. I will enter his hall as the guest of Argus, our mutual kinsman. Every man on earth fears the god of hospitality and keeps his laws."

There was a faint smile on Argus' lips, and a growing glint of respect in his wary eyes. Jason knew he had hit a truth. Every people, however alien, however they feared the stranger in their midst, kept this blood-deep code. Who entered your home and ate at your table had claim to your protection, and you could not harm him; to break bread together constituted a covenant of mutual trust. If you once ceased to honor this, then no man's house was safe.

Jason, standing tall, his hands behind him braced against the ship's rail, looked at them all again. "What say you?"

It was Telamon who spoke first. "Agreed."

"Agreed." The murmur spread with one accord from all their throats, and no one rose to suggest alternative or addition.

"So be it, then!" Elation kindled again in Jason's heart, and a godlike confidence that fermented like new wine overflowing. He threw back his head with triumphant laughter. "So be it! Argus, will you come with me? And your noble brothers?" Argus nodded. "Telamon and Augeias?" They came leaping to their feet, thirsting for adventure. The others, quelling their disappointment in not being chosen, embraced them, slapped their backs and wished them well, and then fell to polishing and sharpening their armory, in case need arose.

"You must come like cats in a fog."

Argus' caution was scarcely needed. In silence, holding their knives in their teeth, the men let themselves down over the sides of the boat into the caressing water. Then through thick-choking reeds, and mud, and rocks, they moved until they reached dry land. All was still bound by mist. Argus moved through it unerringly, his head high and alert, sniffing the air as though seeking some secret signal. By unspoken consent, he had become their leader. He led them surely, along a definite though invisible twisting path, across sand and stones. Presently the path grew steep.

"We climb," Argus stated succinctly and unnecessarily.

"What lies beyond?"

"The Plain of Circe. A sorceress, and sister to Aetes."

They emerged at length upon high ground, not yet free of mist. It stung at Jason's eyes. He peered through it, striding after Argus, not wanting to appear hesitant before this new-found kinsman. Dimly he could make out forest shapes, osiers and willows. They were moving through the rows of a planted grove. From some high branches, shapeless forms hung suspended. Through the fresh mist a half-familiar stench came to Jason's nose. The memory teased his brain; what was it?

Lost in thought, not looking, he stumbled off the path and one of the formless masses grazed his jaw. A roughness of untanned oxhide—instinctively he thrust out an arm to swing it off, and the skin parted. A skeletal foot, bits of flesh still clinging to it, thrust at him.

Jason sprang backward with an oath, feeling his gut retch. "By all the gods, Argus, what is this place?"

"I said. The Plain of Circe."

"More like the Plains of Hades! What are these—things?" Involuntarily Jason's brain was racing. Was this some betrayal? Had Argus destined them for some strange human sacrifice? But no; Argus had broken bread with them aboard the *Argo*.

"It is our funeral custom." Argus was polite but puzzled. "We wrap our men in oxhide and hang them from the highest branches, that their spirits may be free. Thus the air disposes of the dead."

"You do not burn them?"

"That would be sacrilege!"

How barbaric, and how indecent, Jason thought with distaste. Still, what was one to expect of foreigners? And Argus had been kind enough.

"Augeias and Telamon have the same thought," Jason thought, grinning. He noticed that they stuck close behind him, although there was bravado in their walk.

There was good reason to stay close together now. They had emerged from the forest with its grisly burden. The path grew wider, and presently was paved. Stone shapes of buildings hovered close on either side, occasionally a figure passed them, huddled against the mist.

"We are almost there." Argus' murmur might have been only a faint breathing in the mist. Jason stopped and, despite the damp, flung off his wrap.

"We shall not come before Aetes like refugees, but like the sons of kings and gods." He stood as he had stood that day in Thessaly, clad in leopard skin, the muscles rippling beneath his sun-tanned skin and his hair a golden glory down his back. Augeias and Telamon looked at each other, and they too removed their cloaks.

Argus smiled wryly. "A triumphal entry?"

Jason grinned. "Why not? Apollo is with us. Look!" He flung his hand before him, and at that moment, almost at his bidding, the mist parted, the sun sent arrows through the high canopy from a sky of magic blue.

The sun was like an artist's finger, touching and gilding. . . .

"By holy Apollo!" Jason breathed, and was for once struck dumb.

The palace loomed before them, high above, of a perfection unbelievable in this wild country. Rows of soaring columns surrounded the palace walls, and wide gates stood open on an empty courtyard. High over all, a marble cornice rested on triglyphs of bronze.

Jason looked at Argus and was disconcerted at Argus' knowing smile. He sees too much, Jason thought, turning away to mask embarrassment.

The gates were unguarded, and they stepped unchallenged across the threshold. Within was wide and spacious, like the central square of a city. Vines covered with greenery rose high in the air, and from beneath them four springs gushed forth. Ahead was another, inner court where Jason could see decorated galleries to right and left, and folding doors leading to many rooms. At angles to this court, on either side, stood other, higher buildings.

"My mother's house." Argus had seen him staring. "Another is her sister's. The third, the home of Apsyrtus, Aete's pride and heir. The highest is grandfather's own. Grandfather, obviously, is not yet out. The servants aren't about." He cast a disapproving glance around the silent court.

"Someone is." Jason's glance was caught by a moving figure on the gallery. Instinctively, his hand went to the dagger in his belt. Behind him, Argus chuckled.

"My little aunt. Now what keeps her at home? Usually she is busy all day at the temple."

Like a deer startled by unexpected sound, the slight figure started and poised, motionless in flight. For a moment she appeared to Jason like one of Medusa's victims, turned to stone, the flush of young blood still staining the tender skin. No marble statue, this, for the skin was olive gold, and the black slanting eyes shot out strange rays of flashing golden light. She was slim as a youth, but more fragile, little more than a girl. Only a child, Jason thought with a careless glance. Then eyes met eyes, and the gold light scorched his soul, and in a whirling second his destiny was forever altered.

The slanted eyes widened, the startled head flung back its burden of jet hair, and a cry burst from her lips.

"Who calls?" Another woman's voice, older and deeper. A clatter of spindles dropped to marble floor, the patter of women's sandalled feet. The gallery was filled with maids, all in a flurry, interrupted by their mistress running down the stairs.

"Argus, my son!"

"Chalciope!"

The familiar sounds of reunion and a mother's scolding swirled around Jason and he heeded not. Eyes clung to eyes, held by invisible webs. Then Argus clapped him imperatively on the arm, and he wrenched himself away, and when he looked back a moment later, the girl was gone.

"Mother, mother." Argus, ruefully smiling. Chalciope scolding. The other son crowding in for her embraces. Jason, waiting, hoped he did not look as awkward as Augeias and Telamon who were trying to appear like non-observers. Chalciope turned to them then, folding her arms in the familiar affronted gesture of housekeeper caught off guard. Argus, too, turned all charm.

"Mother, greet Phrixus' kinsmen. They have saved our lives."

"Hmph. Had you stayed at home, your lives had not needed saving. But you, you are young, you have to seek adventure. Like these youths, too, I warrant. With no thoughts to your neglected mothers! Now I see Fate has turned you back. How I have suffered! This blind obedience to your father's death wish, and this mad dream of Hellas! My misery, my heartache!

A widow, abandoned by her sons for the sake of an estate!"
Jason hid his smile. It was a very familiar moan.

"Your grandfather," Chalciope said firmly, "will have some
words to say about your misplaced sense of duty."

"Aetes," Argus retorted, "would be the first to understand.
And here he comes."

How had he known? Jason had heard no sign. Yet in the
instant, the empty courtyard had sprung alive with life. Brutish
peasants busied themselves over the great carcass of a bull;
others chopped wood; others heated water in a great cauldron
over an open fire. None looked towards the strangers, none
paused even a second in his labors. They were working, their
industry proclaimed loudly.

The king was among them. No sound, no signal, only that
sudden wave of energy that signals the fact that authority is
present. He stood at the top of the stair, his queen beside him,
imperious, austere, strange in his stone-embroidered, oddly
shaded clothes and grey-gold skin. His eyes were slanted, narrowed, under sharp strokes of brows, and his eyes were cold.

Argus and Chalciope, perhaps for his sake, Jason realized
now, had spoken Greek. Aetes shot forth a single questioning
syllable in a strange tongue, like wild birds crying. Argus answered it in kind, more lengthily. Then his brothers, sturdily;
then Chalciope, placating. Jason understood that the king was
questioning the strangers' presence and that his grandsons were
testifying he had saved their lives. The king nodded, once.

Over the first hurdle, Jason thought; we are in. Now what?
He glanced towards the far gallery again, but the girl was not
to be seen. Only a flutter of bright veil eddied from behind a
marble pillar.

Aetes stretched forth one arm in an imperative gesture, and
it was answered by a cacophony of birdcalls from the peasants
round the fire. He turned and strode back into his palace, his
queen beside him, and the peasants swarmed around the
Greeks, pawing at their garments, muttering gibberish.

"Now what?" Jason cried out hastily to Argus.

"Baths," Argus said. "Clean garments, which these curs think will be a decided improvement on what you wear."

Baths! What Elysium. The water was steaming, and fragrant with fresh herbs. He, like Augeias and Telamon, followed Argus' unself-conscious example and permitted himself to be stripped and scrubbed by a high-cheeked peasant girl. Then fresh water, poured over him from a bronze urn giving forth clouds of steam. Then he was wrapped in fleecy cloth and patted dry by the same girl, who squatted at his feet and rubbed his calluses with pungent oil. Finally robes, strangely cut, embroidered with stones and interwoven with exotic feathers were brought, and oil for the hair, and jag-toothed shells with which to comb it.

Augeias was enjoying himself. "What price your slaves?" he called exuberantly to Argus, who only smiled austerely. "Or perhaps when I am home again we can establish a trade between my land and yours. Your females could teach our women something of how to take care of a man."

But it was over Jason, with his golden hair, that the slave girls fluttered, uttering strange laughs and running their fingers through it. He thrust them from him and moved towards Argus, adjusting the unfamiliar clothes around his body and recognizing the feel of his own muscles and hot blood beneath them.

"Argus, that girl. The little black-haired girl on the gallery when we first entered. Who is she?"

Argus turned, lifting a sardonic eyebrow. "My mother's little sister, suckled by her along with my youngest brother. Not one of the slave girls, and of no use to you in other ways, so be warned."

Jason felt himself reddening. "And why is that?"

"She is vowed as priestess to the witch goddess, Hecate."

"And her name?"

"Medea."

THE
DARK
WOMAN

III

THE GOLDEN
STRANGER

M EDEA-A-A!" The plaintive, scolding birdcall
echoed down the gallery as the old nurse called,
lumbering in search of her charge. She was too
old and crippled now for such searching, she often said. She
had been wet nurse to Queen Eidyia and to Chalciope, although too withered for that role at Medea's birth. "Medeaaa!"
She was Medea's private fury, that one, and she saw too much.

Medea darted from behind the pillar where she had hidden,
watching the strangers' coming. Down the gallery, through the
marble rooms of her own apartments, she fled to the one place
where no attendant dared intrude, her private shrine to Hecate.
"I wish to meditate. Let no one enter!" She flung the words at
her twelve young maids, her closest companions, virgins like
herself, as they swooped around her, twittering excitedly of the
foreigners' arrival. Medea thrust them from her, escaped into
the sanctuary of the small low chamber, and pulled the curtains
tightly shut. Then, in cool shadows, she leaned against the wall,
head back, eyes closed.

By the dark goddess, what has come to me? A golden

stranger had looked up, eyes had met eyes, and an arrow shaft had pierced her breast, as hot as fire. She trembled with it, all else forgotten; her heart, brimful of a new agony, throbbing within her and overflowing with the sweetness of the pain.

No strangers came to Colchis, not since the legendary day when her sister's husband Phrixus had seemed to drop among them from the heavens. "He came among us like a golden god," Chalciope had said. *Like this one now.* But that had been before Medea's birth, and Phrixus was long dead. None had come since; Colchis was too remote and Aetes' mistrust of foreigners too well known. *What would Aetes do now?* These strangers had come with the protection of Chalciope's own sons. *Aetes had thought them gone for good, and he had not been sorry.* Aetes was wary of strangers and strange ways. *Beware of them, for they are not like us.* Her old nurse had told her tales of Phrixus' coming, how country women had covered their eyes from the awful sight and muttered incantations; how Chalciope, told she was being forced to wed this demigod, had feared to look upon him. *She, Medea, had gazed just now unveiled, and the strangers' eyes had devoured and possessed her.*

With shaking hands, Medea lit incense in the burner. Then she flung herself face-down before the sick-sweet smoke. *Hecate, dark goddess, what is this that tempts me to break my sacred vows? Goddess of the Crossroads, do I stand at one now? Oh, Hecate, Goddess of Dark Night that hides my blushes, do not let the stranger die!*

Outside the curtains a furor was commencing. The nurse's strident tones rose above the twittering of her maids. "Child! Where is the girl? Aetes demands your presence. You are summoned to a feast with those barbarians. Indecent, I call it! Medea, you come out of there or I will enter!"

Medea came. She submitted bemusedly to being bathed and anointed by her maids, and dressed at the nurse's instructions in ceremonial robes. But inside her head, seemingly so far away, her brain was racing. *What did he see when he did look on*

me? Her nurse, who was a shrewd old thing, discouraged
vanity, but the reflection in the bronze panel told her she was
not unpleasing. Not to Colchian eyes; she had the high cheekbones and slanted eyelids of their Eastern heritage, and skin
with the rose-olive sheen of bronze itself. But these aliens were
all gold. Her hair was pitch-dark, a heavy weight against her
slender back. The nurse bundled it up, preparatory for the
priestly headdress, jabbing in hairpins. The tension, the flicker
of pain, was almost pleasure. Two maids brought the silver
gown and she lifted her arms, closing her eyes, feeling it slither
into place against her bare skin. Her body was not ripe like
Chalciope's, it was too obvious that she had just emerged from
girlhood. But it was a woman's body, she insisted to herself
with passion. She had never been so aware of it before.

"My paints." A little girl, youngest of her maids, brought the
carved chest, and Medea knelt before the bronze to line her eyes
with kohl and paint her lids from the shell of pigment the child
held out.

The nurse eyed her with disfavor. "Too much."

"Be still."

"I will not. Are you a priestess or a wanton that you paint
your face so for these barbarians?"

"I said be still!" Medea swung out her arm, and the little girl,
struck by accident, screamed and fell backward. The shell
crashed to the floor and shattered, and the child, weeping and
ashamed of it, crept away behind the other speechless maids.
The anger spent itself as suddenly as it had come, leaving
Medea frightened at its power. She turned, unwillingly, to the
old nurse's inexorable gaze, and their eyes locked.

"You see?" The old woman's voice was quiet. "I have told
you that you must not surrender to these fevers."

"My fevers, as you call them, if I have them, come from my
goddess." But Medea could hear the uncertain note in her own
voice.

"Do they?"

"You angered me. I did not mean to hurt the child."

"I am all right, Lady!" The child had scrambled up, trying bravely to stop her crying, adoration in her eyes. "Ooh, Lady, you are so beautiful!"

"There, you see?" Medea faced the nurse defiantly.

"As for beauty, what is that? Sweet poison, and often the poisoner himself becomes afflicted." The old eyes narrowed. "As for the rest, this passion was conceived in a seat unknown to Hecate. Don't turn that innocent look on me, young miss, I know you well. This is not for you, mistress, so be warned."

"I know not what you speak of!"

"Aye, you do. Your face goes rose and white and rose again, and your thoughts leap like sparks from brushwood piled on a smouldering log. And I know where they leap to. See to it it's your thoughts only that do the leaping!"

Medea swung around, eyes flashing, but before she could speak, the old woman had signalled to the maids. They were imprisoning her in the heavy headdress and the feather cloak, hung with the symbols of her joint offices as priestess-princess. Impossible to toss one's head, to strike out an arm, when thus weighted down, and they both knew it. The nurse smiled at her grimly and stumped off.

Medea had thought she had grown accustomed to the garments' heaviness in the few years since she had been initiated into the virgin priesthood. They had set her apart, and she had gloried in it, gloried in the power she sensed she held even over Aetes who, though within the family he professed himself above superstition, nonetheless seemed half fearful not of her magic but of some power she held as yet untapped. Today the garments, and all they stood for, were heavy on her shoulders, and her body in its silver wrappings ached to be naked and free as a child. No, not as a child.

She turned to the door of her apartments, her head high, balancing the great bird headdress, and moved onto the gallery, her maids behind her.

Below, in the Great Court, the banquet had been spread. Slaves bustled everywhere, piling animal skins on couches, spreading forth platters and urns and ewers of honeyed wine. Argus and his brothers stood in the midst of it, and with them the foreigners, looking less odd though awkward in Colchian garments. Their leader was set apart by the golden blaze of his hair, still rippling down his back rather than clubbed in the Colchian fashion. He was speaking with Argus, his back to her, but still she stopped, feeling the throbbing arrow within her breast. At once, as if sensing her gaze, he turned. She had the satisfaction of seeing him start, struck by the splendor of her presence. Good! He saw her now as princess-priestess, set apart beyond ordinary women. He was properly impressed.

"But I don't want to be different!" The childlike thought burst through, unbidden. Not if different meant shut off, untouchable.

At that moment, like some magic she had not thought to bid, his eyes cleared. She saw recognition come. With it, a corner of his mouth curled up as if in secret sign between them, and the blue eyes twinkled.

Oh, he had a magic too, this stranger, which even as it stripped and bound her, filled her with a strange fascinated confidence of being known. *Lady Hecate, what is happening?*

"Lady, Lady, he is not for you." The nurse's murmur, low and dark as a night bird's, was at her elbow, threatening the spell.

"Hold your tongue!" Medea hissed, longing to toss her head. But the headdress held it rigid.

A flurry of ceremonial birdcalls came from below, and a great rustling. Aetes, awesome in his royal robes, with her mother Eidyia on his arm, had entered from his palace door. He frowned, seeing Medea's empty place, and shot a glance up toward the gallery. Head high, her feathers whispering, she descended the stairs, followed by her maids. Aetes held out his hand, she placed hers on it, he swung her to her place. Then, with a curt nod, the king occupied his own high couch and the banquet began.

Medea crumbled her food, hoping to escape the notice of her father, if not of the nurse. Somewhere, behind the pillars of the gallery, those old eyes were spying! She could not bend her head, but she dropped her eyes, glad that the headdress wings masked the changing color of her cheeks. The strangers ate, she saw, darting sidewise glances. They spoke courteously in a dialect of Greek she could just understand, but at times she noticed glances exchanged between them over an unfamiliar dish or taste. Aetes too was watching, his eyes narrowed. They rested longest on the gold stranger and on Argus, though Aetes did not speak. Courtesy demanded that a stranger's physical needs be satisfied before questioning.

At last the slaves brought platters of native fruit, refilled the wine cups, and withdrew backward on their knees. Aetes stretched back upon his elbow and gazed hard at his grandsons.

"Sons of my daughter and of illustrious Phrixus, how comes it you are back in Colchis? What cut your journey short? You would not listen when I warned you of its hazards. Yet now you are back. Tell me plainly what occurred and who your companions are."

A hush had fallen, and Medea saw the golden one and Argus exchange uneasy glances. *Now we are for it,* she thought. This is Aetes' real meaning: *"Why have you violated our isolation and brought in the hated stranger?"*

Argus was capable of a honey tongue. "My lord, that ship of ours, rottenest of all the Colchian craft as luck would have it, was smashed to pieces by the wind and waves. We clung to a plank and were cast ashore on the Isle of Ares, in the pitch-dark night."

"How is it you escaped the war-god's birds?"

"They had been driven off the day before by these men, who gave us food and clothing when they heard your mighty name."

"Why come they here?" The questioning was falling into the formal ritual of the court, a facade, which more than once had served to contain and channel anger. Medea bit her lip and leaned forward, breathless.

Argus' eyes narrowed, but he answered frankly. "They come, King Grandfather, in quest of the Golden Fleece."

A hissing like a nest of snakes filled the still court as breaths were sucked in sharply. *Fool!* The word screamed silently in Medea's brain. *In speaking that you betray the strangers to their deaths. Yet you side with them, else you would not have brought them here. Why can you not learn to be wily as our serpent?* Her pulses throbbed, and her temples went hot within the intolerable headdress. Then in the instant, as often happened, her head cleared. Everything seemed very light and bright, and she could see Aetes' mind.

"He wants to kill them. He is furious, but he has trapped himself by the ritual of this banquet. The strangers have shared our bread, and Aetes dare not risk the wrath of the gods by turning on them. Or, rather, he dare not risk having the people find out he does not respect the gods." Medea knew it as surely as if she had heard her grandfather speak the words.

Oh, but he had guile, did Aetes; all of which she herself had inherited and Argus had not. He sat immovable, walled in by silence, as Argus expended himself in a torrent of words.

"Pelias, an unlawful king who has seized this man's rightful throne, has sent him here on a desperate quest. They maintain that the House of Aeolus—the house of my father, Phrixus— will not escape the wrath of Zeus and vengeance for my father's sufferings, unless the Golden Fleece returns to Hellas. Athene herself built the strange ship they sail on, which holds together in any gale that blows and travels as sweetly manned by oars as she runs before the wind. Those oars, Aetes, are wielded by the greatest and most glorious youth of Hellas. And they come not to seize by force, but to offer fair exchange, to fight in your behalf against our deadly enemies, the Sauromatae."

Argus paused, looking at Aetes, who responded not a flicker. Medea's lungs were hurting. How odd; she had not known she held her breath. The strangers were poised breathless, too, with the relaxed stillness of a coiled cat waiting for the spring.

"You may wish to known these visitors' names and families." Argus had begun again. "They are all sons or grandsons of immortal gods. This is my own kinsman, to whom the others all have rallied. Jason, son of Aeson."

Jason. Medea scarcely listened as Argus continued with the lineage of the rest. Her gaze was all on Jason, but he did not respond; his eyes were fixed on the still figure of the king. It was a stillness growing mixed with fury, and as Argus began claiming for the visitors immortal ancestry, the dam broke. In one swift movement Aetes was on his feet, eyes blazing.

"Enough! Out of my land at once! It was no fleece that brought you here, but a plot to seize my power and my realm. Had you not eaten at my table, I would tear out your tongues and cut off both your hands. Talk not about immortal gods. It is all lies!"

A youth, the one called Telamon, leaped to his feet and was thrust back by Jason.

"Great Lord." Jason's voice was respectful and honey-sweet. "I beg you forgive this momentary violence. In truth, we do not come with the aims you think. It was the Fates, and the brutal orders of a ruthless king that bring me here. If you deign to help me, I will make all Hellas ring with Aetes' glory."

Aetes' eyes had narrowed and their blaze gone out. It was a sign Medea recognized with a sinking heart. Violence was giving way to devious means, and Aetes was a master of deceit.

"Speak no more. If you are children of the gods, or otherwise my equals and no pirates, you can easily meet the test I put you to. And if you do, I give the Fleece to you freely."

A trap. Medea concentrated all the force of her thinking on Jason's downbent head. *Listen, and watch for dangers, and be wary. Aetes will not give up the Fleece. It is his sign of power.*

"On the Plain of Ares, I keep a pair of bulls, bronze-footed, breathing fire. I yoke and drive them over a four-acre field, then sow the furrows with a serpent's teeth. From those teeth spring up an army of armed men; these do I slaughter. All this I can do between the rising and the setting sun. If you can do the same, you may have the fleece."

The king ceased speaking, and there was a great stillness. A long while Jason stared at the floor. Then at last he spoke.

"You leave me no choice, and no escape. I accept your challenge, though it may bring me death. Necessity is the harsh mistress that drives me now."

His voice was quiet and politic, but desperation lay beneath it, a desperation Aetes' answer was not calculated to reduce.

"Go; join your men. If you hesitate in the task you have accepted, I will deal with the matter in a manner to make other strangers shrink from following you here."

His meaning was clear. Jason rose, followed by his two countrymen. After a moment Argus too went with them, signaling by a jerk of his head for his brothers to remain behind. They walked the length of the court towards the great open doors, four young men moving through Colchian antagonism that swept over and around them like the waves of Neptune's sea. Jason, the golden stranger, was at their head, set apart somehow from all the rest. Behind him, as he walked in silence down the long court, Medea turned wondering eyes upon him and her heart smouldered with pain. As he passed from sight, her soul crept out of her like a frightened bird and fluttered in his steps.

STRANGERS'
MEETING

THE GOLDEN STRANGERS were gone. The pageantry of the formal presentation was at an end. And Aetes, it was abundantly clear, was filled with fury. Chalciope, to escape his wrath, hastily gathered her sons together and withdrew to her own apartments. In all the turmoil Medea stood alone, left like a frightened child.

No, not a child. Nevermore a child, her heart told her fiercely. It was no small thing to be proved a woman when she was yet so young. Yet it had happened swiftly and completely. Even within the great feathered cloak she felt exposed and naked, too vulnerable to knowing eyes. Too fragile, for certain, to encounter the shrewd suspicions of her nurse.

Imprisoned by the symbols of her office, Medea walked, as swiftly as she was able, up the stairs and to the privacy of her own rooms.

"Out!" She gestured imperiously to her maids, and her dark eyes flashed, and the young girls crept out, frightened by her mood. Like lightning she slammed the heavy door and threw the bolt. She leaned against the bars, shuddering with the force of her own emotions, and the splendid cloak slid from her shoulders and lay at her feet like a molten pool.

The great bird headdress pressed intolerably upon her temples. With difficulty she lifted it off, and as it came her hair fell free and cascaded around her half-bare shoulders. Loose, unbound hair, uncut, symbol of her virginity. But inwardly she felt no more a maid.

The honey-sweet words of the golden stranger rang in her ears, and all the whole scene in the palace hall flashed diamond-bright before her eyes. How he had looked, the things he said, the way he sat, the very clothes he wore. The way he had walked so proudly to the door, unbowed by the dreadful magnitude of Aetes' challenge. But most of all she remembered the moment on the gallery, when she had known herself ravished by his eyes.

Weeping, Medea threw herself across her bed.

"He is going to die. There is no escape, for if the bulls do not kill him, Aetes surely will. Why do I cry? He is hero or villain; what should it be to me? Oh, Hecate, sovereign goddess, let him live! But—if he must die—let him know I grieve!"

At length, worn out by weeping, she fell asleep. But after a brief time even that sweet oblivion was denied her and she fell prey to the nightmares of a soul in pain. She dreamed that the stranger took Aetes' challenge—not for the Fleece, but to win her as his bride. The pictures flashed and changed; it was she, not Jason, who stood so terribly alone before the raging bulls. Wonder of wonders, they bowed before her, they knelt like docile heifers to her yoke, and she rose with joy. Jason ran to embrace her. But her parents, arms outstretched and angry, barred their meeting. It had not been Jason who had dared to yoke the bulls; he had failed their challenge. He could not have her.

An angry dispute arose in her dream between the Colchians and the Argonauts. The scene changed; they were in the palace hall. Colchians and Minyae, linked in ranks, and the silence hung between them like withheld blows. They were waiting, waiting for her to choose. And she, Medea, priestess-princess of Colchis, without an instant's thought, had turned her back on her parents and walked to the golden stranger.

Behind her back came her parents' screams of anger, and with these cries she woke.

Her body was trembling violently with fear. Medea sat up dazedly, trying with frightened eyes to pierce the darkness. But the pictures were gone, the walls of her own apartments surrounded her, and she was alone in an intensity of desire and fear that filled her soul with terror.

"The coming of these strangers means catastrophe for us all! And oh, you gods, how I shudder for them!" Not for them, but for their leader. "He should be safe at home, courting some foreign girl in his own land." No, she could not bear it!

The thought rose suddenly of her sister, Chalciope, who had wed a golden stranger and who had in time, Medea knew, come to love him deeply. Chalciope, the mother of mixed-breed sons who obviously had sided with their newfound kinsmen and in so doing had incurred Aetes' wrath.

If Chalciope, her beloved sister, asked for her aid as witch-priestess for Argus' sake, her helping Jason would be an act of charity, not of betrayal.

Just as she was, in bare feet and translucent undergown, Medea ran to the door before doubts could assail her. Yet once across the threshold, shame swept down. For a long time she stood there motionless, then at last crept back into her room like a frightened child. Thrice more she tried, impelled by the strange new desire that burned within her, and thrice was driven back, overcome by shame. After the fourth attempt she threw herself face downward on the bed, her body twisting with pain.

"*Why?* I am Medea, priestess sworn to Hecate, daughter to Aetes the great! Why should I feel like . . . like . . ."—her breath caught. Like an unbedded bride whose newfound love has been with harsh swiftness torn from her eager arms. Medea buried her burning face in her pillows and wished to die.

"Sister, dear." Chalciope had come. Chalciope sat beside her stroking her feverish head with loving hands. "Your little maid came and told me that you wept. What mean these tears? You are sick with misery."

The words tumbled to Medea's lips, only to be swallowed back by painful modesty. Chalciope straightened, her voice apprehensive.

"Medea, what is it? Do you know something I do not, some terrible doom that awaits me and my sons? Our father's anger at Argus goes beyond all reason. By all the gods, I wish there was a way I could leave this city and live at the world's end where no one has ever heard of Colchis!"

Medea gasped at the words, so close an echo of her thoughts. Her heart was bursting with the need to speak, but the words could not force themselves through the locked gates of her lips. At last she was able to make a devious reply.

"I weep for terror for your sons, Chalciope. I slept at last, and in my dreams such visions came as I dare not speak. The gods keep such evil from you. But oh, Chalciope, I am so afraid our father will destroy your sons, and the strangers with them!"

Chalciope stared at her, face ashen. "So are your fears my own, though mine has been a waking dream. That is why I am here, in hope that you and I together can find some way to prevent this horror from becoming real."

The first move was made. The tight band around Medea's heart loosened slightly.

"First swear!" Chalciope dropped to the floor beside her, gripping Medea's hands tightly in a vise of iron. "Swear by the immortal gods that what I say will be forever secret between us, and that you will join with me in my cause. I beg you, not to stand idly by while my sons are put to death. If you do, I swear I will die with them and forever haunt your nights like an avenging Fury!"

And she burst into tears and threw herself in her sister's lap. Chalciope and Medea wept for each other's grief, and the sound of wailing was heard through all the palace.

It was Medea who was able first to speak. "You leave me speechless. How can I ease your heart? I wish I could promise safety for your sons. I swear by the most solemn of our people's oaths, by Earth and Heaven themselves, that I will aid you to the utter limits of my powers."

"Then can you not—for the sake of my sons—devise some ruse to aid the stranger in the trial?" Chalciope gave Medea a slantwise glance. "He needs you as much as do my sons. Indeed, he has sent Argus to me to plead with you for your help."

Medea's heart leaped within her, and she could see Chalciope but dimly through her tears of joy. She turned away to hide the crimson of her face. "I will do anything," she said carefully, "that will make *you* happy. May I never live to see another dawn if I put anything before the safety of you and of your sons. You are as much a mother as a sister to me, Chalciope. Now, go! Tell no one what we have spoken. At dawn I will go to the temple of my goddess, with a potion to charm the bulls."

And Chalciope was satisfied.

The world was veiled with the gentle shadow of the night. Sailors far out to sea looked up to see bright Orion and the ever-circling Bear. In the town, men called no more to one another, and no dogs barked. On the *Argo,* Jason, reassured by Argus of Medea's aid, slept the sleep of peace. The darkness deepened, and silence reigned.

No such blessing visited the young girl pacing alone in the darkness of her room. With Chalciope's leaving, shame and horror, those twin torments, had swept down on her like the avenging Furies. Her mind was tortured with guilt at betrayal of her father, and her body yearned for Jason. A searing pain shot deep into the nape of her neck like Eros' arrow, she was possessed by agony, and tears ran down her cheeks.

"Evil on the one side, evil on the other, and how can I choose between? Oh, if only Artemis the virgin huntress had shot me dead before my eyes beheld the golden stranger."

The picture rose before her inexorably—Jason on the Field of Ares, facing the relentless bulls and meeting an ignominious death. How could she endure it? How could she prepare the drugs without her parents' knowledge? It could not be right to betray her father, her country and her gods. She would rather die. No; she was a princess; she must live, and endure with dignity whatever fate the gods would send.

"If it is his fate to perish in the unploughed field, then he must die. Oh, I am born under an unlucky star, for there can be no happiness for me whether he lives or dies."

There was no escape. If she did not give the stranger magic, he would die. "And I will, too," she thought passionately, "of grief." If she tried to aid him, and they failed, then both would die; Aetes was relentless and Medea had no illusions about his parental love. Should they succeed, what then? He would return to his own city and she would be forever marked as a girl who had betrayed family, faith and homeland because she was insane with lust. Better to die at this moment, unnoticed and unreproached.

She sprang up before her courage could fail her and fetched a small chest inlaid with curious designs of bronze. It fastened with a clasp she alone could work and none else dared touch; here she kept her drugs and salves and moonlight-gathered herbs. Among them, Medea well knew, were deadly and swift-acting poisons. Death could come quickly, without pain, and Hecate would welcome her in the underworld as a virgin sacrifice. Her trembling fingers fumbled with the clasp, then stopped.

For hours she sat there like one turned to stone, the box upon her knees, and the hot tears ran unguarded down her cheeks. In those moments she was a child no more, and life seemed a sweeter thing to her than it ever had before.

There was no help for her; whatever happened, she must die.

Very well; then Jason, the stranger who had put knowledge in her heart, would live.

She set the box aside and rose, irresolute no more.

Again and again, soundlessly, she opened her door in the hopes of catching the first glimmer of the dawn. At last, heart pounding, she saw the first faint light flush the eastern skies with pearl. Swiftly, Medea bound up her disordered hair and washed away the stain of tears. She bathed herself with an ointment nectar-clear and drew on a gossamer golden robe. It fastened with curious brooches; as she clasped them, she thought suddenly of Jason's fingers fumbling at their catches, and flushed hotly with shame and joy. She threw over her head and shoulders a shimmering silver veil.

The dawn was rosy now, and her chamber was filled with the fragrance of spring flowers. Softly she called to the twelve young maids sleeping in the antechamber beyond her door.

"Awake! Yoke the mules to my carriage, for I go to the temple to sacrifice to Hecate."

As they did so, still drowsy and flushed with sleep, she took a magic ointment from her box. She had made it from the saffron-flowered plant, which sprang, it was said, from Prometheus' ever-falling blood. One midnight, clothed in black and seven times bathed and purified, she had drawn off the plant's dark sap in a Caspian shell, and the earth had shaken and rumbled beneath her feet and the heavens themselves had thundered with Prometheus' torment. Such was the salve Medea chose for Jason.

She hid it in the scented girdle bound just beneath her breasts, and passed through the sleeping palace and stepped into her wicker cart. Two of her young maids mounted with her, one on either side, and the others tucked up their skirts above their knees and ran along behind as she flicked the light whip and the two white mules trotted off obediently on the broad highway out of town.

Like Artemis, fresh-bathed and in her golden chariot, Medea

looked; and on either side of the road as she sped along, the people, just rising to their morning chores, turned aside and did not dare to meet her eye.

Medea was silent as she sped along, but her mind teemed with plans to deceive her maids. At last she settled on an ingenious ruse. When they reached Hecate's splendid temple, standing alone upon the fertile plain, she stepped down quickly.

"I have done wrong," Medea said. "I forgot my father said it was dangerous for women to venture forth today when the foreigners are everywhere throughout our city. However, since we are here and undisturbed, there is no reason to deny ourselves some pleasure. Let us sing together, and gather meadow flowers, and return to the palace at our accustomed time. And if you will fall in with my plan, you shall have something better than flowers to take with you."

Medea paused. Yes, her tale went well; it accounted for any tremor or vagrant blush. "You must swear an oath not to reveal a word I say. The princess Chalciope has begged me, for her sons' sake, to protect the stranger in his mortal combat. I have pretended to fall in with the idea; indeed, I have sent him word to meet me here. If he brings gifts, we will divide them among ourselves, and he shall receive in return a drug more deadly than he dreams. What I ask is that you leave me alone with him when he arrives."

Her maids heard her, and believed, for they did not dream that she would betray her homeland or her oath to Hecate.

Medea made pretense of casting aside her care, tucked up her skirts, and seemed to sing and dance freely among her maids. But all the while, as the sun rose shyly, her thoughts were fixed on one thing only. Time and again the gay melodies quickly ceased to please; over and over her light-stepping feet faltered to a halt and her eyes turned aside to search the distance. Once she mistook the sound of the breeze for a stranger's footfall and came near to fainting.

A nearby poplar flaunted its leaves to the newborn morn,

and the crows that made their home in it flapped their wings against the glowing sky. A chill ran through Medea, but she flung her head back and laughed defiance. Then she stopped still, and for a moment her heart ceased beating and a warm flush stained her cheeks. A mist veiled her eyes and through it, shimmering in the sun, she beheld Jason striding through the flowery fields.

No hero of old, no son of Zeus himself could outshine Jason on that golden day. Never had he been so fair to look on, so fascinating with his charm of tongue. Brilliant and beautiful and full of danger he sprang to view like an alien god. Like Phrixus, descending on golden rays of sun from the clouds of heaven.

Medea stood motionless, her feet rooted to the ground. Behind her the twelve young attendants disappeared. Steadily he came towards her, the golden stranger. Now they stood face to face. No word, no sound; the very air, time itself, hung motionless between them and dared not breathe.

Jason was first to speak, turning on the full weight of his charm.

"Why are you afraid?" His voice was gentle and sounded to her ears like the chiming of strange bells from a far-off land. "I have come alone. You need not fear I will not respect your virtue, or your youth. I know you are a priestess, and no woman has had cause to fear me, even in my own land. We meet as friends, on what is holy ground. Believe me, you may speak freely, and ask or tell me all you wish."

He paused, but she could not reply. Presently he spoke again. "You have already promised to give me what I need. I beg you, do not put me off with pretty speeches. By your goddess Hecate, by your parents, and by Zeus himself, god of strangers, I plead your help for one who is by necessity both suppliant and stranger. Without you it is impossible for me to achieve success. Give me your aid, and in the days far off I shall sing your praises in a distant land. So will my comrades, too, and their wives and mothers who now sit by a far-off shore, weeping bitter tears which you alone can wipe away. Think of Cretan Ariadne, young as you and like you reputed granddaughter of the Sun. She did not hesitate to befriend Theseus in his hour of trial, to save him from the horns of the dreaded Minotaur and afterwards to sail with him far across the sea. For this she became the darling of the gods. So will you also, if you save me and my noble friends. But you need not speak. I know such outward beauty must be matched inwardly with a tender heart."

His honeyed words melted the invisible wall that held her still. Medea turned away, but her vagrant lips betrayed her with a smile. Then, casting shame aside, she lifted her face and looked full in his eyes. There was so much she longed to say that she could not find speech. Her heart pounded, and in the tight-bound girdle the jar of magic salve pressed like an arrow-point against her breast. Silently she drew it out, placed it in his hands, and thrilled at the joy she saw leap into his eyes. His need for her warmed her heart.

Their glances locked, then sprang apart as at the touch of some strange fear. One moment both stared at the ground, the next their eyes fastened upon each other as though impossible to look away. They could not cease to smile. Speech is safer, Medea thought, than this. She began to chatter rapidly. "Hear me. After my father has given you the serpent's teeth, tell him you must have until tomorrow to purify yourself. At midnight, alone, go forth in somber clothes. Bathe in an ever-running stream, then dig a round pit in our mother Earth. There sacrifice a ewe, and burn it whole, pouring on honey and offering prayers to Hecate. At once withdraw, and do not dare to look behind whatever comes."

Medea shuddered, hearing in her mind the footfall of Hecate and the keening of her dreadful hounds. Then Jason touched her shoulders, sending a current through her, and she went on.

"When morning comes, strip, and anoint your body with this

charm. It will make you feel the equal of the gods themselves. Anoint your weapons also, and you will be vulnerable to neither the flames of the bulls' breath nor the spears of the earth-born men. The charm will last for one day only; nonetheless, you need and must not flinch from whatever comes."

His hands slid down her arms to clasp her own and she turned them in her fingers, tracing the calluses of the past month's hard rowing. "With these strong hands it will not take you long to yoke the bulls and plow the stubborn fields. I see you sowing the serpent's teeth in the dark moist earth, I see a race of giants springing up. Watch, and wait. At the last moment before they see you, fling a boulder in their midst. They will fall on one another like starving dogs and kill each other off. Then will come your moment to plunge into the fray, and you will win. You will carry off the Fleece to your homeland, far away. Go then, where the winds of your fancy take you, when you part from us."

She stopped and was silent, her head bent from the vision of his bright ship sailing, and the warm tears ran down her cheeks and fell onto the ground. Then shame no longer mattered. She lifted her face, taking his right hand in both of hers.

"Remember, if you ever reach your home. Remember Medea's name."

"Of one thing I am certain," Jason answered gently. "Never by night or day shall I forget you, if I live to reach my home. It is a rich land, ringed by lofty mountains, and most people there have never heard of Colchis. Yet it is said it was from here that our ancestor Minyas came long ago. Perhaps my coming, and my winning back the Fleece, will forge a bond of friendship between our people, just as Minos at length was reconciled to Theseus through the love of Ariadne."

He had said too much; the spell was broken. Medea turned away, possessed with bitterness and fear. "Perhaps in your country people honor their agreements. Aetes the king is not that kind of man. Do not speak to me of friendliness to strangers. Remember me, when you are back in Iolcus. Alive or dead, when you forget me, I will know. Then may the storm winds blow me to you, that I may remind you that on this day I saved your life, though it costs my own."

And the tears rained down her face, and Jason laughed. His laughter was like a strange and longed-for music, and for a moment she thought he was going to seize her in his arms. She waited, half-fainting, but the moment passed. Instead his words themselves enfolded her like a caress.

"Lady, lady! You can spare the wandering winds! You are speaking nonsense! Sail with us to Hellas, and you will be honored as goddess by both the women and the men. And I shall build a bridal bed in the royal palace, which you and I shall share. Nothing but death's dark shadow shall ever part us!"

Medea's heart melted within her like wax beneath the sun. Yet at the same moment a tremor ran through her frame. The sun was high, and the meadows rippled as though the very flowers were growing restive.

"We must go," Jason said. "Your maids are waiting. The sun will set before we know it, or some passers-by may see us. We will meet each other here another time."

She longed for him to embrace her, but he turned, head tall, and strode off like a joyful Apollo through the rippling fields of grain. Medea stood trancelike, watching. When her maidens gathered around her like twittering birds, she did not even notice, and as she stepped into the wicker carriage and drove off behind the docile mules, she neither knew nor saw. Her thoughts were all on Jason.

THE
TASKS

A FTERWARDS, it was to seem to Medea that she had left her wits behind her in the flowered golden fields, that some maddening goddess must have bewitched her brain. No sooner had she reached her own apartments than Chalciope was with her, driving away the maids, questioning her in an anxiety of torment about her sons. But Medea neither saw nor heard. She sank down on a low stool at the foot of her couch and rested her cheek on her left hand. Tears rained down at the memory of her infamy, of how she had given way to betrayal and dishonor through the trembling lash of love.

Evening came. Beyond the Ethiopian hills the sun sank below the darkening world, and Artemis harnessed her silvery chariot, the moon. On shore and ship and palace men fell to sleep. Yet Medea lay wakeful, her mind's eye following Jason through all the ritual of preparation she had prescribed.

As in a dream, she saw the solitary figure, like a thief, set out across the silent plain at that hour when the very air was still. Argus was with him on the ship, she had heard that much of Chalciope's anxious murmurs; Argus would have fetched for him the pure milk and the ewe for sacrifice. But that dread journey to Hecate, Jason would take alone, unguarded save for her prayers.

She knew the very lonely spot he would find in the meadow beneath the midnight sky. Her face grew hot as she pictured him bathing naked in the sacred river, throwing about himself the night-dark mantle, which, unbeknownst to her, had been the gift of the deserted Hypsipyle. Now he would dig the pit a cubit deep, now cut the docile victim's throat and lay her carcass on the wood piled high. Now the kindling, now the pouring of libations and the call to Hecate . . .

At last day broke. The rising sun glittered on the distant Caucasus' frozen peaks. As Medea rose, the very bones of her body ached in torment. She bathed and put on again the gleaming golden gown. Her hand trembled as she tried to paint the line of black along her swollen eyelids. With a cry, she flung the polished liner from her, and the frail jade snapped and broke. To her dismay she saw the little maid holding the paint chest involuntarily cower from an expected blow.

It was the child whom, in her torment, she had knocked to the floor two days before. Medea pressed her hands together tightly and her voice was quiet. "You may go. I shall finish later." With astonished gratitude the little girl scuttled away.

From the distance Medea heard voices, hurrying feet, the sound of preparations. Aetes had the palace stirring early. A knocking at the gates, and a steward's voice, announcing: "Telamon, favored of Ares, and Aethalines, son of Hermes." Jason's messengers had come to receive the serpent's teeth.

By right she should be sitting quiet and proud awaiting the appointed time to ride with Aetes to the Plain of Ares. By right she should be praying for the stranger's ignominious defeat. Waiting was intolerable. Already at this early hour the sun's white heat was invading the marble walls, pressing down upon her like the weight of the feather cloak. Medea went out onto her private rooftop and bent forward, trying to draw fresh breath into her hurting lungs.

Far off on the distant shoreline, small figures moved. The

Argonauts, too, were astir with preparations. A circle of forms surrounded a solitary figure—Jason was anointing his weapons and body with the magic salve. Now the others rushed at him, testing his weapons, but they did not break. The gigantic Idas, in a seeming fury, hacked at Jason's spear with his great sword, but the blade rebounded. From the distance, a great shout of joy went up.

The drugs Medea had infused in the olive-oil salve were penetrating Jason's skin; she saw him leap in the air again and yet again, like an exultant war-horse eager for the battle. His bronze shield and his ashen spear flashed like lightning beneath the beating sun.

He was ready; the small figures streamed back onto the boat, and Medea knew he had given the signal to depart. Like a toy ship, *Argo* began to move upstream towards the Plain of Ares.

Below her in the palace, a bronze gong sounded. The old nurse stood in the doorway, eyes shrewd and knowing. "Aetes waits."

Two of her maids were holding up the feathered cloak and others held ready the great headdress and the jewels of state. Medea swung round to her nurse in panic. "Not today!"

"This is an official occasion, your father says. You must bless the Colchians as their priestess. The strangers seek to carry off a national treasure."

"I cannot. Say that I am ill."

"I will not." The old woman grasped her by the shoulders as she tried to turn away. "One can do what one must. Remember that."

Her voice was stern but her face, as she searched Medea's eyes, was anxious. Impulsively Medea reached out and touched the wrinkled cheek in a rare gesture of affection. Then she turned and submitted docilely, like a sheep dumb before the altar, to the weighting down of the robing, the investiture and the setting apart.

At last she allowed her maids to lead her down the stairs and out the heavy doors. The white heat struck upon her like a blow. The state chariot waited, its horses snorting and pawing the ground. At the reins stood Aetes, splendid in warlike glory. He had put on his bronze breastplate and set upon his head the golden helmet with its four plates bright as the faces of the sun. In his left hand he held his shield of many hides, and in his right the mighty spear, which no Argonaut save Hercules could have withstood. By his side stood Apsyrtus, who was all his pride.

It was difficult to mount the chariot weighted down by the heavy cloak. As she did so, Aetes shot her a dagger glance. Medea gazed back unflinchingly, reminding him she was priestess as well as daughter. She held herself erect, disdaining the rail, as Aetes took the reins from Apsyrtus' hands and they galloped off down the broad highway toward the Plain of Ares. As they came, the thronging crowds opened like an aisle before them and then came hurrying after. The Lord of the Colchians rode forth like Poseidon to contest the Golden Fleece. And overhead the white sun blazed in the brilliant sky.

The Colchians were first to reach the trysting place. Rank upon silent rank their men lined up along the Caucasus Mountains' rocky spurs. Before them Aetes wheeled and turned his gilded chariot along the riverbank.

Chalciope came hurrying to Medea's side. Behind her, to Medea's relief, hovered her four sons. Somehow in the dark hours Argus had managed to slip back unnoticed from the enemy camp. That was well; soon enough Aetes would discover betrayal among his own blood kin. Medea's heart pounded in her breast, and her lungs hurt with an intolerable pain.

"The strangers' ranks are troubled," Chalciope whispered. "The giant Idas wants to seize the Fleece by force. But others, Peleus and Telamon, and the sons of the North Wind and Meleager, the courageous youth, all stand with Jason. As for our father, he has determined that these men are pirates, and means after their leader has been killed to burn their ship and every man alive. If the stranger does not win his trial, all will surely die."

Medea closed her eyes to shut out the throbbing sun, and her temples burned within the priestly headdress. Then a sound like the cry of birds swept through the Colchians around her, and she opened her eyes, and beheld the strangers coming. They flowed from the bank-moored ship like a shining river, in silent rows, dressed in their finest, like the sons of gods and kings. The purple plumes danced proudly in their glittering helmets, and the hot light of morning glinted fiercely on their spears and shields. But Medea's eager eyes could not find among them the face of the golden stranger.

Formally, as in a ritual, Aetes handed the reins to his proud son. He gestured once, imperiously, and slaves leaped forward to lift off the cloak and crown of office and unbuckle the brazen armor. As man, not as king, Aetes stepped, without deigning a downward look, from the golden chariot. His muscles rippled beneath his dark skin and his slitted eyes were proud.

He strode forward and dragged out the adamantine plow and the yoke so heavy no other man could lift it unassisted. Another gesture, and from some smoky stronghold in the earth two bulls burst forth. Their bronze-shot hooves ripped up the ground, and from their yellow nostrils came breath like fire. Aetes in silence forced them to the yoke, and the furrow he ploughed was straight, it clove the earth a fathom deep. From the Colchians another cry arose. Aetes released the bulls, and they thundered off to the place from whence they came. Then Aetes, magnificent in his own strength, turned to the strangers.

"This I can do, and plow the four-acre field and sow and then cut down its crop of armed men. All this alone, between the rising and the setting of the sun. Let now your king do this, the captain of your ship, to prove himself worthy of the Fleece that glows with skeins of matted gold."

Silence fell, and the fierce white sun beat down on Minyae

and on Colchians alike, and all men waited. Then the ranks of
the strangers parted and through the aisle that cleared for him,
Jason came. He carried with him a sharp-toothed helmet of
shining bronze, and from his shoulder his sword was slung.
But he had thrown off his saffron clothing and strode like an
athlete, his body bare and proud. His skin, bronzed by the
journey's sun, gleamed with the oil of the magic salve so that
he shone like Apollo of the golden sword.

Neither to right nor left he glanced, but went straight to the
yoke and plow where Aetes had cast them down. He drove his
spear into the earth and leaned his helmet on it. With shield
alone he went forward to examine the tracks the bulls had
made. Then he straightened and turned, planting his feet apart.
He stood, and waited, and no signal passed, but from the
bowels of the earth there came a rumbling as from Hephaestus'
forge, and the earth seemed to open and the bulls plunged
forth. They charged wildly, and terror swept the assembled
crowds. And over it all the hot sun burned.

Fiercely the bulls bellowed, and they butted against Jason's
firm-held shield, but he shifted not an inch. With his hands he
seized the horn of the bull upon his right and dragged it to the
bronze yoke, and with a sudden kick brought the great beast
humbly to its knees. In like manner he felled the second with
a single blow, then he cast the shield from him and held the
beasts down with his own strength. And the deathly heat
assailed them from all sides.

Together the twin sons of the North Wind lifted the heavy
yoke, and Jason bound it tight around the great brutes' necks.
Then he lifted the bronze pole between them and fastened it by
its pointed end. Now his twin assistants backed away. And
Jason, all eyes upon him in the silence, slung his scalding shield
upon his naked back, and picked up his heavy helmet with its
proud plume and the long spear he had brought from his far-
off home. Like a Pelasgian god, he drove the spear into the
flanks of the bulls.

The breath of the mighty beasts came like roaring fire, and they leaped in fury. But firmly Jason grasped the handles of the plow and drove it surely. To the right and the left the huge clods fell, torn groaning from mother Earth. As he followed the sure plow, planting his feet down firmly, Jason cast the serpent's teeth from him to the furrows left and right. And the bulls thrust their bronze hooves into the earth and toiled steadily on, and the hot sun shone.

At last only a third of the passing day remained, but the plowman's work was done. Jason halted, unbound the bulls, and they fled, bellowing, across the plain. A murmur of awe and anger traveled through the Colchian ranks. In the golden chariot Aetes, speechless with rage, howled a wordless cry of grief. But the solitary laborer paid no heed.

The Minyae stretched out their arms to Jason and ran to gather around him as he came to meet them. They gathered grass to crown him, and their sweet words were like caresses. Jason dipped his helmet in the flowing river and drank deeply. Then he straightened and turned, and across the whole empty length of the Field of Ares, ringed by silent watchers, his eyes met Medea's dark slanting ones with their gleam of gold.

In the high chariot Medea still stood straight and tall, supported by her robes of office, but she was near to fainting. The golden gown clung damply to her body, and the rays of the merciless sun drove like pincers into her brain. Then Jason's eyes impaled her, and a moan escaped her parched lips, and she almost swayed. And from the ring of watchers, Minyae and Colchians, arose a cry.

Medea closed her eyes, and opened them, and all things swam before them in the burning sun. Was it hallucination from those blinding rays, or drug-caused vision, or magic, or some miracle of intervening gods? She neither knew nor cared, and the very question did not arise to her bedazzled brain. Yet suddenly the empty field was filled with the rising up of many men. An earthborn race of warriors, brazen-armed. The descending sun flashed hot upon them in all its splendor. Medea watched, trancelike, as one carved in stone.

Like a golden god splendid in his strength and youth, Jason advanced. He lifted from the field a heavy boulder and, like an athlete with a discus, flung it into the army's midst. From the Colchians arose a shout like the roaring of the sea, and the earthborn men with mighty cries began to fall upon one another with swords and spears. But Jason the confident stayed at the edge of the field and crouched unseen behind his golden shield. And the white sun burned, and those two flames danced hypnotically before Medea's dazzled eyes.

Like pines before a gale, the earthborn army fell. And now a bright meteor leaped among them, leaving a fiery trail. The son of Aeson blazed through their midst with sword unsheathed. And the furrows of the fresh-plowed field ran red with blood, until in the still heat of late afternoon an army of the dead lay like felled saplings after a torrential rain.

In the gold chariot, Medea closed her eyes and drew a breath that filled her lungs with pain. Aetes in black silence wheeled the horses round and galloped back to Colchis by the quickest way.

And the sun set, and Jason's task was done.

ELOPEMENT

THAT WAS a night, if ever one there was, when no light should shine. But the fickle, treacherous moon rose high. It glowed like molten silver, brighter than the yellow light that burned in the council chamber where Aetes plotted treachery with his nobles. Its slender fingers invaded the apartment where Medea paced alone, and she knew that Hecate, her dark goddess, had withdrawn her blessing.

"She knows I have betrayed her. So will Aetes know, when his rage cools and his brain turns in coldness. There is no safety, for myself, or for the others while they are here."

And her heart was filled with an agony of fear.

"What if my maids heard what was said in our secret meeting? What if they tell?" Aetes had ways to end all silence. The thought made her tremble like a young deer trapped by the baying hounds. Her ears roared, and her eyes burned in an anguish no tears could quench.

Her cornered mind could see but one escape. With shaking hands she lifted to her lap the bronze-bound chest and opened the compartment where she kept her deadliest drugs. There was escape here, quickly and with little pain. Fragrant hemlock, cool with the scent of her beloved woods, that led one gently, quietly to sleep—her fingernails broke the seal and she closed her eyes, lifting the phial with both hands to her frightened lips.

Stay; wait—all was not completed. Jason had not yet secured the Fleece. Her wiles had carried him safely past the bulls and the armed men, but she knew with a certitude past all factual knowledge that Aetes would never allow him to freely take the prize and go. Never, unless he could seize the Fleece now, just now, and steal away in night shroud, could he be safe. She could not escape into everlasting sleep and leave him alone to face Aetes' wrath.

"I need not think of Argus and his brothers. They stayed with Jason at the ship; he will take them with him . . ." If he left; if he left now, at once; if he could find means to achieve the Golden Fleece. And if he did . . .

"Sail with us to Hellas . . . you will be honored as a goddess. And I shall build a bridal bed. . . ."

Medea poured the drugs back into the chest with hands that shook no more.

There was much to do, and little time, for the night was now far spent. She could take little, lest if she be observed her unnatural burdening caused her to be stopped. But the chest could go; people were used to seeing her abroad at night to gather drugs and perform her secret rites. She flung a wild glance around the far reaches of the room. The golden gown in which she had first met Jason . . . she dared not wear it; hastily she made a bundle of it and the silver veil and her favorite jewels. At the last she added to them a delicate crown of gold, fine as thread and curiously formed into gem-set flowers. It might be the bridal coronet for a virgin priestess. . . .

No more of that! Swiftly she stripped and pulled on the dark garments she wore in the rites of Hecate. They would be least noticeable by moonlight, as well as providing reason for her journey. She flung over herself a black, all-concealing veil.

It was done. Medea, poised for flight, paused for a final look. Here in this quiet chamber she had dreamed the dreams of girlhood, here sat up all one night in terrified expectation before her initiation into the rites of Hecate. Her old nurse had been with her then; now, she could not even say good-bye. She could make no farewell to her mother, that lovely awe-inspiring queen, nor to Chalciope, who had nursed her at her breast with her own sons.

In sudden trembling passion, Medea flung herself against the wall. One hand crept down it softly, memorizing its texture, the crack where once in a fit of temper she had flung a metal cup. She kissed the pillars on either side of the folding doors and caressed the twisting golden snake that formed the foot curve of her bed. Her fingers ran with trepidation down the curtains that veiled the entrance to her private shrine, but she did not go in. She turned, and threw back her black veil, and tore off a lock of her unbound hair. This she laid across the bed, in memory of her girlhood, and said her last farewell.

And so she left. The very doors of the palace sprang open to her, unbidden, at her touch. Barefoot she picked her way among her sleeping maids and past the guards; barefoot she ran behind the palace down dark alleys thick with filth. With her left hand, she held her black veil to hide her face; with her other hand, she lifted the hem of her somber skirt. This was a secret way she knew, through the mean streets and gutters of the city, which she sometimes took by dark of moon to gather herbs, or when a lonely longing she did not understand drove her to Hecate's temple. Tonight the moon burned like white fire, and Medea understood all that she felt.

As the moon burned for Endymion, so Medea burned for Jason, and her ears rang with the gods' ironic laughter.

She knew this way well in the concealing dark and had come here often, fearless. Tonight the silver light revealed to her its ugly secrets, and she shook with fear. But nonetheless her pounding heart impelled her on. At last the walls of the city, with its threat of watchman's discovery, lay behind. Ahead the dark woods, sacred to Hecate's mysteries, loomed. The roots and branches and noxious weeds, which she so often gathered, reached out their twisting arms, but she gathered her cloak about her and moved on. Her breath pained her, and she did not dare to pray.

Then the woods fell away, the moonlight glowed serene. Medea stood alone in the sacred meadow where she had stood with Jason, and round about her feet white flowers glowed like fallen stars.

Here, but a short bit ahead, the riverbank rose high, and on its opposite shore a fire glowed. The Minyae celebrated with its blaze the single-handed triumph of Jason, son of Aeson. Nearby, her prow kneeling on the shore, *Argo* rocked gently in sweet sleep. At the sight, a shuddering relief swept through Medea that broke her iron control. She swayed and almost fell, but summoning all her strength, she sent ringing across the river a clear call.

After minutes that seemed like hours, figures moved. By the flickering light Medea recognized the youthful form of Phrontis, Chalciope's youngest son. He knew her voice and turned in swift amazement to rouse the others. Now his three brothers stood beside him, and then a fifth figure. An Apollo with golden hair.

Three times she called, and thrice back the answer came, and all the while *Argo* moved toward her with steady speed, propelled by the noble rowers' stalwart arms. Even before the hawsers were made fast, Jason leaped like Hermes from the deck to the pebbled shore. He was followed by Argus and by Phrontis. Sobbing and stumbling, Medea ran down the bank and threw herself at their feet, her arms around her cousins' knees.

"Aetes knows. He has guessed all, and you must flee at once on your golden ship, and I with you, for if I stay here I shall surely die."

The men were stunned to silence at her outburst. In the secret recesses of Medea's mind the flame of pride, nearly quenched in her self-abasement, flickered again to life. She flung back her tear-stained face and looked the lord Jason directly in the eyes.

"Let us sail at once, before the king can even have his chariot ready. I myself will lull the guardian snake to sleep and put into your hands the Golden Fleece. But I call upon you now, before your comrades, to affirm to the holy gods the vows you made me. I have left country and kinsmen, trusting a stranger's word."

So Medea spoke, and she saw in Jason's eyes that which told her she had touched his heart. With both his hands, he reached out and took her own and lifted her to her feet. He gave her, tenderly, the embrace she had so longed for. Then, calling his companions to witness from *Argo's* prow, he said, "I swear by Olympian Zeus, and by Hera, Goddess of Marriage, that when we are safe in Hellas I will take you into my home as true-wedded wife." He swore as well that nothing but death would part their love, and he took Medea's right hand in his own to seal the covenant before gods and men.

Swiftly then they took Medea on board their ship, and with all speed pushed off from shore. Behind them, far in the distance, the moon's rays touched with silver a lofty roof. The roof of the Palace of Colchis . . . of a sudden, like the lightning, the realization of all she was putting from her stabbed Medea's heart.

"Never again will I see the shores of home, or kneel at familiar altars. Henceforth and forever I shall walk a stranger among strange men." In wild regret she ran to *Argo's* stern and stretched her arms out to the receding shore. But Jason ran to her, and imprisoned her in his arms, and with words of re-assurance blotted out her desperate yearning.

They reached the shore of the Plain of Ares at that late night hour when the wise hunter ventures forth before the glare of dawn. Here they landed on the very ground where the Ram that carried Phrixus had first stretched his weary knees. Nearby stood the smoke-grimed altar where Phrixus had sacrificed his golden saviour. Here, at Argus' bidding, Jason and Medea alone were set ashore.

Before them lay the challenge field Jason had plowed and sown. Beneath their feet the clods still bore dark stains like blood.

"Come." Medea held out her hand. She led Jason after her along the path to the sacred grove. The darkling wood at first concealed its awesome treasure, but as they approached she felt Jason's hand tighten on her own and heard his swiftly suppressed ejaculations of surprise.

Before them, deep-hidden in the holy grove, a clearing opened. In its center rose a giant oak, and its highest branches, like outstretched arms, held up. . . .

"So it is true," Jason whispered in a tone of awe.

The great Fleece hung like a tethered cloud burning gold with the fire of a rising sun. Through the dark night of fear it glowed and put the moon to shame. Medea stood close by Jason's side and tried to see the scene with stranger's eyes.

Round about the great tree's roots its serpent guardian lay. At sight of the stranger, it stretched its long neck and raised itself up high. Its monstrous length of horny scales twisted and rolled like a forward-surging wave. A hissing terrible to hear came from its open throat, and the deep woodlands and high riverbanks threw back the awful sound. Far off, babes sleeping in their mothers' arms awoke and were hugged tighter to their mothers' anxious breasts.

After the first shocked moment, Jason's hand went swiftly to his sword.

"No!" Medea's frantic strength tugged his arm away. She sprang forward, flinging herself against the monster's girth. The twisting stilled, and a strange sound of contentment emerged from the serpent's throat.

"He is my friend, and he is immortal. You must not hurt

him!" Medea fumbled in her bosom and brought out a homely jar. "He knows each night I bring him supper. He is very fond of honey. See?"

The serpent's forked tongue licked eagerly at the jar she held. Medea settled on her knees beside him and caressed his head. As he feasted, she began to sing, and strange was the song she sang. Birds twittering sleepily in the trees ceased their own music, and on the forest floor wild creatures stopped their rustling and grew still. Medea's sweet young voice wove a cobweb spell, invoking Morpheus, the god of sleep. Slowly the whole length of the giant snake relaxed, his undulations smoothed like one silent swell rolling over a dark night sea. His eyelids drowsed, then opened.

Medea bent, and whispered in his ears a magic spell. The scent of her perfume dazed him. Picking a sprig of juniper, she dipped it in her most potent drug, which she sprinkled on his eyes. And the fragrance enveloped the guardian snake, and sleep fell upon him, and he stirred no more.

Medea turned to Jason, her finger on her lips, and gave him one swift gesture. As swiftly Jason ran to her side, leaped over the serpent's coils, and to the tree. Up and up he climbed, until he tore from its lofty branches the Golden Fleece.

Like a silent cat he dropped to the ground and began at once to bound towards the silent ship. Not until he was halfway through the woods did he realize he was alone, and turn, impatient. Medea had thrown herself across her beloved pet, still stroking the wild one's head with magic salve, and lamenting her treachery with scalding tears. Jason had to return and urge her with outstretched hand. Only then she rose, put her hand in his, and without word or backward glance left forever the somber grove of Ares.

Out on the open footpath, moonlight claimed them. It shone on the dazzling Fleece in Jason's arms, and he held it high. His hair shimmered in the reflected golden glow, and Jason's face glowed also, alive and exultant. Medea, watching, was reminded of how she herself was wont to dance, finding pleasure in catching glinting moonlight on her silken gown. The days of such innocence seemed long ago, but she took joy now in Jason's joy. When presently he flung the Fleece across his shoulder, it reached the ground, and the very earth where he walked was bright with gold.

They reached *Argo* just as dawn spread her blessing over the sleeping world. And all the young men marveled when they saw what Jason brought. They leaped to touch it, but Jason held them off. He made a careful bundle of the Fleece, and covered it with a new mantle of finest wool. Then, taking Medea's hand, he led her to a seat and turned to address his men.

"Let us embark without delay for home. The prize for which we greatly dared is ours, and easily so, thanks to this gracious lady whom I will make my wife. You too must cherish her as the saviour of you all.

"But now our need is speed, not eloquence. Already Aetes' barbarian troops will be hurrying to bar our open passage to the sea. To the oars then, two men to each, taking turns to row. Those with free hands will hold aloft our ox-hide shields, to protect our brothers and ourselves from the strangers' arrows. In our hands now lies the future of our country, our aged parents, our children yet unborn. All Hellas waits. Will we plunge her into grief, or bring her glory?"

With that he donned his helmet with the purple crest, and held high his flashing shield. And as one voice his eager comrades responded with a shout. Jason drew his sword, and with one stroke cut through the ropes that bound proud *Argo* fast. Like a lord of battle, spears in hand, he stood tall between Medea and Ancaeus, and the ship leaped forward as the men at the oars strained every nerve.

In the bright heat of morning, *Argo* swept in triumph down the widening river and into the open sea. Medea plucked Jason's arm.

"Look there!"

Colchians in multitudes were streaming to the riverbank, numberless as storm-whipped autumn leaves. Above them towered Aetes in his chariot. His left hand held a rounded shield, his right a torch of pine. His great spear pointed seaward, and by his side stood Apsyrtus, son of the Sun.

Jason's face darkened. "He meant to burn us."

"Too late now. We have reached the sea!" And from the men of *Argo* a great cry rose. An answering cry of bitter rage thundered from the Colchian horde, and Aetes lifted up his hands in frenzy and shouted his vengeance to the avenging gods.

As for *Argo,* she found a fresh breeze and an open sea. By the third morning, they had reached the mouth of River Halys, and Medea went to Jason.

"Bid your men land here. We must propitiate my Dark Goddess with a sacrifice."

Jason listened, and Ancaeus gave the order, and they made fast the ship on the Paphlagonian coast. There under Medea's direction they raised an altar, but the secret rituals with which she prepared the offering she did not permit them to see. When she returned among them on the waiting ship, her face was pale, but the strain in it had stilled.

"Now you may sail. I have prayed for you a fair wind home."

His shipmates looked to Jason, but Jason said, "How shall we sail? Did not Phineus tell us we were to return to our own country by another way? He said we should have guides enough, but none has yet arisen. His words proved true about the aid of artful Aphrodite; shall we not follow his advice in this?"

"We all have thought," Idas said impatiently. "Not one of us has heard of another route. Already the Colchian horde will have violated the silence of the sea. We must leave at once, by the only way we know!"

He would have continued in this vein had not Argus, son of Chalciope, eagerly broken in. "We will reach Orchomenus. The prophecy has been spoken to us and you alike, and prophecy never errs. There is another route. The ancient priests of our people, who came from Egyptian Thebes, have given proof!"

And the Minyae gathered around the Colchian prince and listened with eager ears to what he had to say.

"In ancient times a king went out from Egypt. Through the whole of Europe and Asia he made his way, and the people traveling with them founded many cities. Some lived, some fell, but to this day proud Aea of Colchis stands, and in its temple are tablets of titanic stone, with maps engraved by our ancestors of their routes through land and sea. There I have seen a river, the furthest branch of Ocean Stream, and it is broad and deep. Far, far away from Colchis its waters rush from the mountains north of the North Wind. One runs down into the Unfriendly Sea, the other south and west to a deep gulf that stretches up from the sea that washes the shores of your own land."

As Argus finished, the sun broke through the lowering clouds, and they beheld across the waters a trail of celestial light. With joy they welcomed it as a sign from the gods of the way that they must go. So they put ashore Dascylus, son of Lycus of the Mariandyni, that he might return by land to his own people. Then they ran up all their sails, and the canvas belled with a fair wind for home. And the wind held, and the heavenly fire to mark their way.

Across the wide Unfriendly Sea the proud ship scudded. Medea stood in the prow, her face uplifted to the spray. Her veil fell away, and her pitch-dark hair streamed like a satin banner in the breeze. She was unafraid of the swaying of the ship beneath her feet. At night she lay alone on the bed the Minyae had made for her of their finest robes, and looked up at the far bright stars above her head, and dreamed great dreams; by day she stood, sensing those dreams come true, and laughed at the Fates like an exultant child. So could she see herself, flying triumphant into the glowing future, with Jason by her side. If she shifted position slightly, her shoulder grazed

Jason's arm, and she knew he was not unresponsive to her nearness.

"Nor I to his," Medea thought restlessly. She closed her eyes and faced with stark honesty the truth she had hitherto managed to avoid. How often in the night she had lain wakeful, listening to the racing of her heart and thinking on things she ought not know. Once she had felt his eyes devouring her through the darkness. He wanted her as much as she did him. It would be no small thing to prove herself a woman, so young, with such a man. Yet something held her back. She was princess, not to be lightly taken and discarded.

"I will marry the son of a king. Wed in red ribbons, and bedded on gold. And all his people will witness our covenant." The words ran in Medea's brain like a joyful hymn. She slid her hand around Jason's arm, lifted him a slantwise glance, and smiled.

Heretofore they had been sailing due west, but now Argus faced Ancaeus. "There are two mouths to the River Ister of which I spoke. Since we must sail north towards the river's source, we should take the northern route." So they changed their course, but the celestial fire still glowed.

Into the river mouth *Argo* sailed, between inland mountains and the island called Peuke, and as she went she spread panic in her path. On either shore gathered tribesmen who had never seen a vessel of the sea. They lit fires, and made obeisances to the Argonauts as to passing gods, and Medea flung back her head and laughed for joy.

"Ahead," said Argus, "lies the Cronian Sea, beyond the Rock of Cauliacus. There, on one of the two Brygean Isles sacred to Artemis, let us make camp." Ancaeus nodded and gave the order, and presently the great Rock rose at one side, and they sailed peacefully down the Illyrian passage. Now the wide expanse of the Cronian Sea opened up before them. They entered it with sail and spirits high.

Something glittered before them on the nearer shore. Gold

like massed armor in the waning sun. Jason swung around. Barbaric ships blocked the narrow passage through which they had just sailed. And now appeared, on every shore and inlet, ships and armed men, dark men with feathers bristling from their brazen helmets.

"The Colchian horde . . . the Colchians have outstripped us by the other route." They had posted guards at every outlet up to the River Salangon and the Nestian shore. And Argus dropped his head on his hands and groaned aloud.

Medea grabbed Jason's arm. "Sail!" she hissed. "Sail quickly to the Isle of Artemis for refuge. Apsyrtus fears the hunting goddess upon whose favors Colchian life depends. His men will never touch us there!"

So there they landed and made camp, and swiftly offered sacrifices to the goddess. The Minyae stared at one another and without words began to prepare their arms. Outnumbered as they were, they would die with honor. But Jason rose and flung on his leopard cloak.

"Let us parley first, and we may avoid a battle. The Golden Fleece is mine by right, since I accomplished Aetes' appointed tasks."

The message went out to the Colchians by the sons of Phrixus, and at night by torchlight Jason, with Argus and a few companions, went from the island where they camped to the nearby island where the Temple to Artemis rose. There he met Apsyrtus.

On *Argo,* Medea waited, paced and trembled, and her heart was prey to fears. Jason was in the right; he had won the Fleece. But she, not Jason, understood the real bitterness that gnawed at Aetes' soul, and knew he could exact a fierce revenge.

At length, when the torches flickered and nearly failed, the little party of Argonauts returned. Anxiously their companions gathered round them as they came on board. Medea stood apart, still as a statue, and her eyes searched the recesses of Jason's mind. The strain had left him, but his face was drawn.

"Apsyrtus agrees. The Fleece is mine, since Aetes himself had promised it if I fulfilled the terms. The means by which I won it do not matter."

"And I?" Medea's words sped to Jason above the Minyae's head like a quiet arrow.

Jason would not look at her; it was to the Minyae that he spoke. "As for the Princess Medea, she has transgressed her vows, and we have taken her with no right from her people. We are to leave her in chancery in the Temple of Artemis. There she will remain alone, until one of the kings entitled to mete out justice in this region shall decide whether she returns to her homeland or follows us to Hellas."

"No!" The words burst from Medea's lips before she willed them. "It is a trick! I sacrificed everything most honored to save your life. You must not desert me to lose mine at their hands!"

Then the incredible was happening. Jason was turning to her like a distant god, full of dignity but devoid of passion. "You must go back. We, royal, must put our own desires aside. For the sakes of both our peoples, to preserve peace and honor, this must not be."

For a moment Medea only stared at Jason, frozen. Then she was flying at him, her nails like claws. It took the combined strength of Argus and Phrontis to drag her from his face.

BLOODSHED
BY DARKNESS

BUT THAT," Argus said flatly, "is, quite simply, that."
He turned to Medea with an unequivocal look. "As
you would see, my little aunt, if you would not give
way to the female weakness of much passion . . ."

Medea, standing apart by the rails, shot him a glance of impotent fury. Argus ignored it and continued. "Aetes publicly
promised a victorious Jason the Golden Fleece. It is no disgrace, but rather to his honor, if he thus awards it, much as we
know it is to his secret loathing. As for me and my brothers—"
Argus' lip curled ironically. "He is well content to be rid of us,
to have us seek the throne of a Grecian ancestor and not his.
But you, dear princess-priestess aunt, you have done the unfor-
giveable. You have destroyed his pride."

He did not need to complete the thought; Medea knew her
father well. Too well; better than Jason. Jason was a stranger,
good and kind, he could not understand. That was it, of course.
Her brow cleared.

Medea turned to Jason where he stood, separated from her
by the width of Argo's deck and by the Minyae gathered round
in conference. She could see him but partly between their

crowded figures, but when she reached out her arm and beckoned once, he came. Perhaps he was glad of rescue and brief respite from the horns of his dilemma. No, she chided herself, don't think that, think rather that he longed to be beside her and dreaded the thought of sending her away. He was a prince of honor, that was why he had spoken as he did. But also he was a man.

Medea took him by the hand and led him towards the stern where they could speak unheard. There in the darkness, lit only by a fitful flickering of a guttering torch, she turned and placed her hands on both his arms, her body curving in to his with instinctive wile.

"Dear my lord, what is this plan you make, you and my brother, to dispose of me? Am I no more than a bauble, carelessly picked up and carried off by a foreign visitor to my royal home? To be as easily returned with glib apology and a conscience clear?" She forced her voice to stay melting soft and tender. "No. I am a woman, and you know it well. And no common woman, but one of royal blood, who has defied convention and her own stern code, abandoned country, goddess, parents—all. And why? For love of Jason."

Jason was silent. She could feel him holding himself rigid, refusing to allow his body to respond.

"I have made myself yours—daughter, wife, and sister. Why are you not ready to stand by me, come what may? Instead you leave me, like a forgotten pet, while you consult with kings. We are equals, pledged to one another before your peers in law and honor. Or has success destroyed your memory of the oaths you swore by Zeus when you sought my help?" It was dangerous folly to throw up to him his debt of gratitude, but it was the only weapon she had left; she had given herself too completely, and Jason knew it. Her dark eyes flashed. "Where now are the honeyed promises that I believed? Abide by them—else draw your sword and slit my throat, sacrifice to my foolish passion and your pride."

She slid down to her knees, her arms hugging Jason's legs, rocking back and forth.

"Lady, I like this business no more than you. But what can I do?" Jason sounded not like a lover, but Medea's sharp ears caught the note of uncertainty in his voice. She had disconcerted him, a tenuous advantage. "We are encircled by a horde of enemies on your account, and fighting would be fatal. Even the natives would side with your brother, thinking him right to lead you home to your father in disgrace. Would that not shame you more?"

Shame was in her now, and self-revulsion. To grovel so, stripped of pride, at a stranger's feet . . . Medea flung back her head and her eyes shot the golden sparks of the Children of the Sun. "How could I hold my head up before my father, whatever way I came? I see clearly now, and I will beg of you no more. I am alone, and far from home, with only the wild seabirds to wail my fate. And why? Because I trusted a golden stranger. May your homecoming be as bitter as will mine. May the avenging Furies drive you from your home, and may the Fleece vanish like an idle dream. You won the Fleece through my own folly. I have disgraced my sex. Now I am nothing in your eyes, but you will learn better soon!"

She was trembling all over, but with rage, not passion. Jason was looking at her with something like alarm. And the realization came with slow astonishment—he was afraid. He, the golden hero, was afraid of her wild emotion. Afraid, and quite rightly too, of Apsyrtus' men. It was true that the native hordes would help her brother; they held dumb notions of women as the property of their men. If only Apsyrtus were not here. The natives did not love the Colchians so much they would risk their own lives for them in a lesser cause.

Medea lifted herself to her feet, her pitch-dark hair falling like a concealing curtain before her face. This behavior was not seemly; it was self-defeating. She must remember her old nurse's teaching, must not give way to rage. Outwardly she was calm, but inwardly, to her own cold horror, her brain was racing.

Aetes had been crossed, and Aetes was unforgiving. The blood of Eastern centuries ran in his veins. There were only two things that mattered more to Aetes than pride of place. His public honor and Apsyrtus. Apsyrtus his heir, child of a different mother than herself; Apsyrtus, Phaethon to his Sun.

She, Medea held in her hands alone the power to join those two in a terrible pattern that could hold Aetes back and let the *Argo* flee.

The vision that rose within her burning eyelids held her in a paralysis of death. Then she opened her eyes and looked full into the face of Jason. And the way was set.

"It is true, then, what the Old Ones say." Her words came slowly, like a bewildered child's. "A deed of evil begets further evil, no matter what we will. Like the teeth of one serpent, from which a hundred enemies sprang. So be it, then; what is done cannot be changed. It was I, blinded by love, who first played false to honor; I who am an embarrassment to your honor now. I see clearly—I think I see clearly—it must be I who saves you now by paying the most terrible price of all."

Jason was staring at her, dumb with puzzlement. He did not understand; he would never understand, and for a moment Medea almost hated him. But it was no matter. Her fate was forever sealed, had been so from the moment she looked down upon him from the balcony. In that moment she knew herself the stronger and more wise, and knew her love for him was a prison that would hold her ever.

When she spoke again, Medea's voice was that of a woman old and hard. "Send for Apsyrtus, tell him that I consent. Offer him splendid gifts. When he comes for them, then you will know how much I do for you."

And Jason listened, and believed.

The word was sent out to Apsyrtus by the envoys: the lady Medea would be set, alone, upon the island sacred to Artemis, and there be left. But Medea spoke in secret to the heralds of her brother. "Tell Apsyrtus to come to me in the temple when the barbarians have gone, and let him come alone. I was taken by force onto *Argo* by the sons of my sister Chalciope, and feared to tell the barbarians it was not my will. But to my brother the prince, I will tell all. He must come to me in swiftness and in secret. I have a plan whereby he can win back the Fleece from the usurper Jason."

Silently in the dark the Argonauts prepared a boat, and as silently lowered it from *Argo*'s side. Medea drew her dark cloak over her silver veil and golden gown. Her face was pale in the light of the fitful torches, and pressed by her side, hidden in the folds of her gown, she carried a secret thing. Jason also donned his prized armor, and the helmet with the purple plumes, and over his shoulders he threw the splendid cloak that had been given him by Hypsipyle. He girded on his golden sword, then he turned and held his arms out to Medea and lowered her over the side into the waiting boat. Four oarsmen came, too, laden with precious gifts. Gifts to seal the treaty with the prince of Colchis.

Like the beat of muffled drums the oars splashed slowly through the darkling sea, and across the waters the torches sputtered and flared on the ships of Aetes, king of Colchis. Medea stood, peering through the blackness, pulling the dark cloak tightly about her, and a chill was in her bones. They beached on Artemis' isle in full view of the Colchian troops and carried into the temple the splendid gifts. Last of all, Medea stepped ashore and walked, a small and lonely figure, towards the deserted temple, and the Minyae oarsmen rowed away. But secretly, under cover of dark, Jason, too had landed. He crept like a lurking leopard, into the blackness behind the temple walls.

Far out across the waters, the flares showed the return to *Argo* of the Minyae lords. Distant oars splashed, and *Argo* moved away. The wind whispered through the trees, bringing to Medea's ears the voices of the night. At last, faint as the whirr of the wings of a night bird, came another sound. She strained towards it, but could hear only the roar of her own pulse in her ears. Had Apsyrtus come, or had he set for her a deadly trap?

The nightboat stopped, and footsteps came, the footsteps of a man alone. Medea trembled, shrinking back against Artemis' pale statue. Apsyrtus, all unsuspecting, stepped into the temple to claim his wayward sister.

He stopped, and saw the precious gifts, and on them, spread finest of all, the cloak of Hypsipyle. Even in the darkness Medea knew his covetous eyes were glittering. He bent, fingering the wondrous stuff, then straightened and in a harsh whisper called her name.

Medea worked a magic so that her voice seemed to come from the reaches of the temple walls. "Lift your faint torch that I may see your face and know who comes." And Apsyrtus turned towards the sound, turned from the statue, and the light from the pitch knot blinded his vision so he could not see what lay behind.

Medea stepped out, and the dark cloak fell away. Her arms swung upward the sacred thing she carried. With the sacred axe of sacrifice she struck her brother down. And she flung before her eyes the silver veil as the blood of her blood kin spurted upon it, dark in the darksome night. Now Jason sprang forth from his hiding place, his naked sword held high. Like a butcher killing a strong-horned bull, he thrust it in the breast of the prince of Colchis, and Apsyrtus fell to his knees on the porch of Artemis, and the sanctuary was polluted by his blood. In his death throes he pressed his hands across the wound, but the dark blood flowed and painted red Medea's silver veil. And so he died, and in the darkness an unseen Fury watched all that happened with implacable eyes.

Jason knelt in the pool of blood at Medea's feet, and three times he licked up the blood of Apsyrtus and three times spat it out in ritual expiation. Then he rose briskly. "We must make haste away, lest we be found. Give me your cloak."

He had to ask twice before Medea understood. Numbly she handed it to him, and in it he wrapped the body of Apsyrtus, using handfuls of grass to stanch the flow from the double wounds. He put around Medea's shuddering shoulders the cloak that had been Hypsipyle's gift of love. Then, shouldering his grisly burden and seizing Medea's hand, he led her by stealth to the island's other side. Here, hidden from the Colchian ships, a small boat waited. In it they laid the still-warm corpse, and Medea crept in also, flattening herself for hiding against her brother's body. Jason took off his armor, and hid it beneath the splendid cloak and waded into the warm sea that washed away the stains of blood.

Then, soundlessly, the small boat pushed away, but no oars moved. It was propelled by silent swimmers to waiting *Argo*. There, unseen, all were drawn aboard, and the body of Apsyrtus with them, and no torches burned. And the sail was raised, and under cover of darkness, guided by the stars, they sailed out of the Cronian Sea through the passage left unguarded by the Colchians in recognition of the truce.

With the dawn, the Colchian horde discovered that their prince was missing, and they came in swift pursuit. In the first ship Medea saw the form of Aetes the king, her father. She steeled herself and uncovered the stiffening body of her brother, picking up again the axe of sacrifice. Like a butcher dismembering a slaughtered beast, she hacked the carcass into many parts. And as the ship of Aetes the king gained upon *Argo*, Medea flung over the side Apsyrtus' head.

As she had known it would, the Colchian ship stopped, turned, and pursued the bobbing trophy until at last it was reverently taken up. Aetes would not leave to the waves and water beasts the body of Apsyrtus, who had been all his pride. The Furies pursued forever those who let the bodies of their kinsmen go dishonored, and the spirits of their dead could never rest until the funeral rites were done. So again, and yet again, at intervals, Medea flung pieces of Apsyrtus' corpse into the waiting waves that floated them to Aetes. And each time the fleet of the Colchians fell further and further to the rear.

At last a thunderstorm arose, and the exultant Argonauts, lifting their faces to the driving rain, acknowledged it to be a gift of grace from Hera. It put to rout all Colchian hopes of overtaking *Argo*. They turned away, and the proud Greek ship sailed free.

Medea stood by the rail in the beating storm and her blood-stained veil clung like a sodden spiderweb against her, and she flung back her dripping hair and turned to Jason.

"The water washes the blood from off our bodies, but not from our heads. By it you know Jason and Medea belong, now and forever, one to the other!"

THE ISLE
OF CIRCE

DAY AFTER DAY the proud ship put to sea, and her sails belled before the welcoming wind. Medea, standing apart at the rail, was learning what other women had before—that for men who go to sea the ship herself is mistress.

She had not known loneliness was to be her companion.

It was Peleus who had determined *Argo*'s course. "While it is yet dark, let us take refuge in some passage in the farther shore. There let us stay until we are sure the Colchians have sailed for home, then we can easily resume our intended course."

So it had been, and *Argo* had been brought to pleasant rest on the Isle of Amber, most inner and most sacred of all the Amber Islands in the mouth of the River Eridanus. After a time, when all had deemed it safe, they had left the Isle of Amber to resume their voyage home. But they found the Cronian Sea so choked with islands they knew not how to thread their way between. So they sailed to the peninsula where the Hyllean people dwelt. The Hylleans welcomed the travelers with signs of friendship, and freely assisted them on their way. And after that the endless days began.

Southward they sailed, down the Hyllean coast, past the Liburnian Isles like a string of pearls, past the dark-forested island sailors called Black Corcyra. Past Melite and steep Cerossus. Presently on the horizon they beheld the silhouette of Nymphaea, fabled home of Calypso of the magic spells. Faintly through the mists they could discern the high peaks of the Acroceraunian Mountain range.

There it was that the wrath of Zeus descended, bringing terror to *Argo*'s crew. A strong wind rose that swept them back, straight back to the Isle of Amber across the Cronian Sea. And the gale raged, and as they ran before it, a fierce cry, like a human voice in torment, was wrenched from the beam of Dodonian oak in *Argo*'s stern. The voice groaned with images of endless wanderings across tempestuous seas, of sufferings for the blood guilt of Apsyrtus' death.

Out of the night *Argo* had spoken, and the strong men heard and wondered, and their hearts knew fear. Then Medea arose, trembling but resolute in the knowledge of her secret powers.

"The voice of the gods has spoken. I am priestess; I tell you what I hear. We must seek absolution. Therefore let Castor and Polydeuces, sons of Zeus, beg the immortal gods to grant us passage to the Italian Sea. There must we seek out the enchantress Circe, the Daughter of the Sun."

At once the twins rose and raised their arms in prayer. But all the others of the Minyae were fallen in despair. And the endless days went by.

Weeks passed, and they journeyed north. Around them mountain peaks rose tall to pierce the brilliant sky. Alone by the rail Medea shivered and pulled Jason's cloak about her, and the winds swept down, crowning her streaming hair with bits of crystal shimmer.

At length they reached a fearsome lake full fathoms deep. From the depths of the dark waters rose clouds of steam, and round the shore tall poplars, whispered an endless, unavailing wail. From this lake the tears of Apollo, mourning his lost son, overflowed in drops of molten amber. From the steam arose a nauseating stench, as of smouldering flesh, and the devout and the superstitious turned away and muttered hasty prayers.

"It is the lake where Phaethon burns since he fell, struck by the bolt of Zeus, from the chariot of the Sun."

The exhausted Argonauts left swiftly and made their way to the deep River Rhone, and from there passed into storm-swept lakes in the country of the Celts. As they were about to enter a great gulf, they beheld, looming before them, a mighty rock, and the broad sky rang with a terrifying cry.

"It is the voice of Hera," Ancaeus whispered, "warning us of wrong turning." And they turned away and sailed on past the lands of numberless barbarian tribes. But no harm befell them, for a magic mist rose around *Argo,* concealing her from any enemies, day after endless day. Medea lifted her face to the fingers of the mist, and her heart knew cold. Then at last they came to where the mouth of the river emptied into the sounding sea, and a warm sun shone.

They passed the islands of the Stoechades, and by hard rowing reached the Isle of Elba. Here they went ashore, and the Minyae cast off their garments and plunged into the sea, then scraped the salt sweat from their bodies with pebbles from the stony beach. Here they rested in the sun, and played at games and quoits, until at length Medea sought out Jason and drew him aside where they could speak alone.

"We must sail on! I tell you, we must seek out Circe and ask her how we can purge ourselves of the guilt of blood. Otherwise we will never reach your home."

Jason relented, and with the dawn they sailed across the Ausonian Sea and came to shore on the famous beach of Aea. There in the first hot rays of sun a strange sight met their dazzled eyes. A golden woman of inhuman beauty was bathing naked in the sea, washing her long hair and her gleaming garments as if to cleanse them from the vestiges of a terrifying dream. Round about her gathered ill-formed creatures, neither man nor beast. The dumbfounded Argonauts drew their breaths in awe.

Jason shook his head as if to clear his eyes of some strange vision. "Looking on these, I can almost believe the tales of how Earth was created from primeval mud."

Swiftly Medea put a shocked hand across his lips that he might not blaspheme. The woman raised her head, and from her dark eyes shot the golden light of the Children of the Sun. So Medea knew it was true that Circe and she were kin.

The woman did not speak, but when she had gathered up her garments she turned to the strangers and beckoned them to her with one sinuous gesture. At once several of the Minyae lords stepped forward, but Jason held them back.

"Take no notice," he said. And they obeyed, and stayed, but Jason himself followed in Circe's steps, leading Medea with him by the hand. When they reached the splendid house, the lady Circe turned. Now it was Medea who stepped forward, her head high like the princess that she was. Eyes held eyes in indissoluble clasp, the gold light flashed, and woman recognized woman as a Child of the Sun.

Wordlessly Circe gestured them to enter and to sit in polished chairs; wordlessly Medea, and Jason with her, sat instead upon the hearth. Medea bowed her face upon her hands, and Jason fixed into the ground his hilted sword, after the manner of suppliants in distress, and neither looked the lady Circe in the face.

By these signs she knew they were fugitives with the guilt of blood upon their hands, and at once she set about the rites of absolution provided by all-understanding Zeus for the killer who seeks asylum at a hearth. A suckling pig she took and, holding it high above their heads, she cut its throat that its warm blood might fall upon their hands. Next she offered libations, calling on Zeus the Cleanser who hears the murderer's prayers. Then her attendants carried from the house the refuse from the sacrifice, but she herself remained upon the hearth, burning cakes and making offerings to Zeus, praying that the avenging Furies might relent and that Zeus himself might once more smile upon the guilty pair.

At last, when all was done, Circe took Medea and Jason by the hand and raised them up, bid them sit on polished chairs. She herself took a seat nearby from which she could watch their faces.

"Whence have you come?" Her voice was low and throbbing like exquisite music. "What has brought you across uncharted seas, and why do you seek asylum at my hearth? For I have dreamed a dream of death and murder, in which my walls ran red with blood, and fire consumed my magic, a fire I could quench only with the blood of a murdered man."

At this the tears rained down Medea's face and she longed to fling herself at Circe's feet. But she answered quietly, as was meet, speaking in the Colchian tongue, which Jason could not understand. She told of Jason's quest and of *Argo*'s voyage, of how she herself had been induced to turn against her father by the pleas of the unhappy Chalciope, how she had fled from Aete's tyranny with the sons of Phrixus. She spoke, though she did not mean to, for the first and only time, of the torment she had suffered in a first and fatal love. She did not speak a word of the murder of her brother. But Circe was not deceived.

"I pity you," she said. "You have indeed wrought a shameful homecoming for yourself, for have no doubt, you will not long escape your father's wrath. He will soon be in Hellas itself to seek his vengeance. But I will not add to your afflictions. I must demand, however, that you leave my house, you and this foreigner with whom you have chosen to link yourself without your father's leave. Kneel not to me, for I can never approve your conduct or your flight."

At the cool words, Medea's grief welled up beyond all bearing. She pulled her veil across her face to hide her shame, but the wail of pain burst from her and she shook with fear.

Without a word Jason rose and took her by the hand, to lead her shivering from Circe's house.

THE BED
OF GOLD

O N THE BEACH of the Tyrrhenian Sea, the young
lords waited and passed the time with archery and
quoits. But the lord Peleus went apart, by the water's
edge, and the sun sparkling on the water made a dazzle in his
eyes. In the blue-gold mist he discerned a slender form, and a
voice like dancing seafoam seemed to come to his wondering
ears. It was the voice of the sea nymph Thetis, who once had
been his bride, and these were the words he heard.

"Long enough have you sat here, you and your gallant
friends. By the light of the next dawning you must sail off; it
is the wish of Hera. She has ordained that my sister Nereids
will foregather to guide *Argo* safely through the Wandering
Rocks. But if you see me among them, you must not speak my
name."

With that the vision vanished and all that remained before
him was the foaming of the sea. Peleus returned to his companions in a daze. To them he passed on the message of his
vision, but though they besought him, he did not call the messenger by name. Nonetheless, the Minyae accepted the author-

162

ity of the words he spoke. At once they broke off their games and began preparations for supper and the night. And Jason and Medea, returning among them with downcast faces, did not demur.

When the next dawn lit the eastern edges of the world, a wind sprang from the west. In high spirits the Minyae weighed anchor. They raised the great sail high and taut in the morning breeze, which welcomed them and carried them along. And none but Medea mourned the words of Circe.

Soon Anthemoessa, that beautiful island, came in sight. This was the home of the bewitching clear-voiced Sirens, who with their sensuous melodies lured sailors to their doom. But Orpheus, the blessed musician, raised his Bistonian lyre. Lively and fast-moving was the tune he played to protect the Minyae's ears from competing sound, and the West wind, aided by backwash from the shore, carried the ship away from Anthemoessa, and so the young lords were saved from the Sirens' harm. All, that is, but one. The mind of Butes the noble, son of Teleon, was so enchanted by the Sirens' lure that he leaped from his polished bench, threw himself over *Argo*'s rail into the sea, and swam off towards the vanishing shore. And the hearts of Argonauts were overcome with gloom.

A further, greater peril lay ahead. Before them on one side the sheer cliff of Scylla rose, while on the other Charybdis churned and roared. This fatal point, at which the two seas met, had often brought the greatest of sailors to their grief, for many escaped the whirlpool only to founder on the ominous rocks. Not far ahead the great seas boomed upon the Wandering Rocks, while nearby flames of lava shot up above the crags where Hephaestus swung his hammers on Aetna's mount. Now, as *Argo* neared, the flames stilled in Hephaestus' forge, and the pall of smoke settled to mingle with hot vapors rising from the sea.

Argo, under the firm hand of Ancaeus, approached with caution, for the hearts of the Minyae were not ashamed to quail before these dangers. Suddenly a ray of sunlight pierced the mist, and through the narrow passage between Scylla and Charybdis an escort came. A school of dolphins gambolled towards gallant *Argo,* leaping and flashing like Nereids in the grey-gold light. They reached the ship to turn and run, surrounding her. Now up they darted, now ahead, beside, behind, and the crew cast off their fear and laughed to see them.

On either side and ahead the dolphins flashed, like an attendant guard, and in their midst *Argo* passed safely through the treacherous straits. Now before them lay the threatening Rocks, and the dolphins began to run along the tops of reefs and cresting waves, like sea-nymphs holding diaphanous skirts high above their slender knees. All around *Argo,* angry seas rose and crashed. She was caught in the current, tossed from side to side. But the dolphins, leaping and twisting, seemed to toss the lovely ship through the air atop the waves, as maidens toss a ball to one another on a sandy beach. The waters swirled and seethed, but *Argo,* staying amidst her dolphin guard, safely escaped the Wandering Rocks.

The passage took as long as daylight lingers on a night in spring. At last the perils lay behind. The fair sail caught the wind, and *Argo* ran swiftly past Thrinacie and the meadows of the Cattle of the Sun. Here the dolphins vanished, diving deep into the sea, and here the Minyae marveled at the idyllic scene that passed before their eyes in the last faint light. The light was failing now; when dark was well upon her, *Argo* was out in the open sea. Dawn found her approaching the reaping-hook island of Drepane in the Ceraunian Sea.

To this rich and fertile island, where it is said the sickle of the Titan Cronos lies deep-buried, *Argo* came. And King Alcinous and his people welcomed the ship and her load of ills with open arms. The whole town feted the Argonauts as it would welcome home its own far-venturing sons. The finest animals were sacrificed, and offerings of thanks made to the gods, and a great feast was made ready for all the people.

Among them Jason and his companions wandered freely, rejoicing in good fortune. All but Medea, who could not be merry.

"Is this how it will ever be?" she wondered. Circe had been right. No need to put further curse or misery upon her; she had doomed herself. Medea straightened, running her sea-wet fingers across her brow before turning back to Jason. Then she looked out to sea, and her eyes grew wide, and in an instant she was running, her skirts held high, heedless of dignity or proper form as she burst among the celebrants around the wine bowl.

"Jason!" She reached him breathless and clung to him for support. "My father's ships . . . coming in across the sea. . . ."

At once the celebration ceased, and swiftly the Argonauts armed themselves against approaching danger. If fighting came, they would not be unready to respond in kind. With their Phaecian hosts, they hurried to the shore.

In across the waters, like the writhing loops of a dragon, came the Colchian ships. It was not the fleet of Aetes the king, which they had met before, but another fleet, which, separating from Apsyrtus at the Unfriendly Sea, had made their way by southern route to meet them here. Nor were these Colchians, even without the presence of their king, slow in presenting their demands. The princess Medea was to be returned at once; there was to be no bartering terms. If the Argonauts did not acquiesce, reprisals would be savage.

Before the general of the Colchians had finished speaking, hands of the Argonauts were on their swords. Already Peleus and Idas were stepping forward, and their fingers itched around the burnished hilts. It was King Alcinous who prevented them, stepping swiftly between the leaders of either side.

"You come at day's end, at a time of feasting. There will be no bloodshed on my kingdom's soil because of a foreign feud. And peace I can enforce, for my own troops outnumber all your arms. Tell me your quarrel, each in turn, that I may determine the justice of your cause, and in the morning I will pass judgement on your plea."

The words brought terror to Medea's heart. With a cry she flung herself at the feet of Arete the queen, touching her knees in ritual supplication. "My queen, my lady, as you are a woman, help me! Do not allow the Colchians to drag me back! You are kind, you will understand it was not evil but a girl's misjudgement that has brought me to my ruin. I thought to help my unhappy sister and her sons, but I did wrong, and it was fear of my father's wrath that made me flee. They will tell you I was possessed by unholy lust, but I swear to you by the Sun and the secret rites of Hecate, I never meant to run away with foreign men. Through all these months, I am still virgin, I have not been touched. Oh, Lady, pity me, soften your husband's heart, and may the gods reward you with children and honor and a happy life in a city free from war."

Her hot tears fell upon the sandals of Arete, and the heart of the queen was moved. She lifted Medea to her feet and whispered words of comfort, but she made no promise. Medea, frantic in her fear, tore herself away and ran to one after another of friends of Jason.

"My lords, you, and the help I gave you, are what have brought this trouble to me. Remember what I have done for you, and do not turn your backs on my distress! For you, I caused the bulls to be yoked and the earthborn men cut down, and incurred my father's wrath. Through me the Fleece like molten gold burns on your gallant ship. Through me, you are homeward bound to life and joy, but I have become a thing despised, dependent on charity of foreigners in foreign lands."

The men turned their faces and would not meet her eyes, and Medea drew her breath in pain. "By all your gods, respect the oaths you made, and fear the vengeance of the heavens if I meet my death! I seek asylum of no fort, no gods, I turn to you alone, and what I find is hearts of stone. Have you Greeks no shame? When you wanted the Fleece, you were ready enough to take arms against all Colchis and the king himself. Where is your bravery now?"

The Minyae, thus appealed to, did their best to allay her fears. They unsheathed their swords and lifted high their spears, promising to stand by her if justice were not done. All spoke but the voice that she most longed to hear. For Jason, with the Colchian general, still stood in parley with Alcinous the king.

Night's gentle mantle descended to put an end to action, and Alcinous' will prevailed. Colchians and Minyae returned to their own ships to await the dawn, and the Colchian horde sailed a fair way out to sea. King Alcinous and his whole train returned to their own homes, and night put the world to sleep.

No such blessed oblivion touched Medea's fevered brain. In the sleeping camp on the shore in the harbor of Hyllus she sat alone. Only a few armed Minyae, chosen by lot to guard the ship, kept company. It was a night such as Hecate would have loved, for no star shone. On a rock by the feeble fire she sat, and her body ached as if her very bones were old. Pain wrung her heart, and though there were no sobs left she let her tears run quietly, like a patient widow turning her spindle in the night, weeping for her lost man and her orphaned child.

When night reached that hour when the lady moon, had she been traveling in her chariot, would have reached her halfway passage through the night sky, a footfall approached beyond the edge of the sleeping camp. With catlike swiftness Medea flung herself into the blackness beyond the flickering light. The guard sprang forward, his sword arm ready, and Medea's heart stilled, for the newcomer's words were Greek, not Colchian.

"I have a message from the queen for your Lord Jason. The Lady Arete has been badgering our king for half the night." The herald from the palace gave a knowing grin. "I dare say she made the bed too hot for him, for he has told her his decision. The queen says to Jason, wed the girl at once and get her straight to bed, for Alcinous will not separate wife from husband, but he will send her back to Colchis if she is yet virgin."

It was not such a wedding as a girl had dreamed.

At once, upon the herald's departure, Jason was summoned, and he came swiftly to Medea's side. There was no asking or answering, for there was neither time nor need. The friends of Jason were kind and well-intentioned; they set about at once, as best they could, to prepare the customary rites, mixing wine with water for the blessed gods, gathering vines and flowers by the light of torches, garlanding a sheep, which they led to the swift-built altar for the sacrifice. All this they showed to Medea, and she nodded her assent.

Only once she spoke, to Jason, in swift stolen private. "Where? Not here, not on the beach. And not on *Argo*." She was trembling, and Jason touched her shoulder.

"There is a cave nearby, called the Cave of Macris, sacred to the nurse of Dionysus."

Medea nodded. Dionysus, god of ecstasy, god of the clouded mind . . . yes, it was fitting.

From the stores of *Argo* the Minyae brought forth their cloaks of fur, and fragrant linen, and of these they made in the cave a bridal bed, and on it they scattered flowers as they remembered brides' attendants doing at weddings they had seen at home. They brought forth dates, figs, honey, and bread to stand for the sesame cake, of which both bride and groom should eat. Medea watched and nodded. These were the rites of Greece, not Colchis; they were not her ways.

Alone she went to the water's edge in the night without a moon, and alone she bathed herself and rubbed her body with sweet oils, whispering the prayers and singing the songs that were her mother's right. Then she clothed herself in the golden gown, and on her dark hair, which streamed upon her shoulders as sign she was a virgin bride, she set her jeweled crown. Over it she flung the silver veil from which the skies had washed the stain of her brother's blood. Alone, garbed in splendor, she came to Jason. And the Minyae, in their finest robes, opened their circle around the fire to let her through.

The fire blazed, symbol of the hearth of home. Beyond its

flames she looked into the face of Jason, and in that moment it was a stranger's face. A stranger, in a splendid cloak embroidered all in gold. She put her right hand on his, and in Greek, that foreign tongue, they spoke the words that bound them one to the other. The sheep was brought forth, garlanded for sacrifice. Its throat was cut, and the blood caught in a golden bowl and sprinkled with wine on the heads of bride and groom. Then they ate together of the cake of bread.

Jason took Medea by the hand, and by the light of torches led her to the cave. On its silver-glinted floor was the great bed laid, and in it spread. . . . Medea caught her breath. The fiery splendor of the Fleece lit up the cave as its skeins of matted gold caught and threw back a thousandfold the light of the flickering flames. Involuntarily she moved, and the faint gesture fluttered the silver veil, stained with the blood of sacrifice and of her brother. Wedded in red, and bedded in gold. . . .

There in the cave the Minyae left them, taking their torches with them as they left. Outside the cave they formed an unbroken rank and faced towards the sea from which the Colchian ships would come. They wreathed their brows with leafy twigs, picked up their battle-spears, and to the clear notes of Orpheus' lyre, they sang the hymeneal song.

The music drifted in through the mouth of the cave and echoed and reechoed from its rocky walls in wave on wave of muted ringing sound. It throbbed like the beating of her own pulse in Medea's ears. The wool of the Fleece was soft against her skin, imbued somehow with a comforting reminder of her childhood, and her heart felt near to bursting with mingled joy and pain. In the soft blackness that enclosed the bed, she threw herself into Jason's arms, and her last bridge burned behind her.

She felt as if she were surrendering herself to a golden god. He felt as if he was being devoured by some dark goddess. And therein lay the root of all that followed. We do not much care for surrenderings and devourings when they are our own.

THE DESOLATE
LAND

W HEN DAWN THRUST her rosy fingers
through the opening of the cave, Medea lay
with Jason sleeping in her arms. His weight was a
burden on her, and she gloried in it. But her heart throbbed
with fear at the thought of the Colchian troops.

Up from the sea they came, and the martial music of their
wood-reed pipers was like warbirds calling. But another music
floated distantly across the waking land, the lyres and sweet
bells from the palace of the king. And yet another sound—
high, magical, insistent—went out to meet them. The voice of
Orpheus, with his Bistonian lyre, singing of the marriage of
Medea to Jason, son of Aeson.

Across the dawning landscape, the people came, and the wedding hymn of Orpheus met them and enthralled them. They
ran to their homes, and ran forth again with presents and rejoicing.

Down from his palace came Alcinous, judge and king, with
Arete his gracious queen beside him. His robes were royal
purple, and in his hand he held a judge's golden staff. Com-

pany after company of Phaecian nobles marched with him, fully armed. Countrymen led the best ram of the flock, and a milk-white heifer that had not toiled, and carried jars of wine. The women brought embroidered robes and ornaments of gold and all the finery to deck a bride. The smoke of burnt-offerings rose in the pearly air, and all the island beaches and dewy paths laughed in the morning light.

The Argonauts were still in their splendid clothes, wearing their leafy wreaths and carrying spears with which they had kept watch through the wedding night. They appeared to the people as heroes from the Age of Gold, and many marveled at the sight. And all the while Orpheus sang his wedding song and beat the ground with his gleaming sandal in time with his ringing lyre.

Colchians and Phaecians and Minyae lords met in the field before the sacred cave. There Alcinous made known his judgement, as he had revealed it to Arete his queen.

"There is no greater king than Aetes, and far away as his kingdom lies, he could bring war to Hellas if he wished. I will not step in to break a contract given, neither will I lightly defy a sentence pronounced by Zeus. Here is my decision, and the whole world will acknowledge it is best. As a daughter belongs with her father, so a wife does with her husband. If the Princess Medea is still virgin, the Colchians shall take her back to Aetes, and no man shall stop them. But if Jason son of Aeson has taken her to wife, I shall not separate them, nor shall I deliver a child of hers to her enemies if she has conceived."

So spoke Alcinous the king. At which Orpheus entered the sacred cave of Macris, and with his magic lyre led forth Jason and Medea, hand in hand. Medea wore her golden gown, and she had piled up her pitch-dark hair with pins of amber, after the manner of the Colchian woman who is no more a maid. On her head she had set her glittering crown. A flush stained her cheeks, but she did not cast down her eyes. She walked straight and tall, as befitted a woman and a queen. As for

Jason, the dazzling cloak of curious embroidery hung from his shoulders, his gold hair rippled down his stalwart back, and together they walked like gods.

In vain the Colchians protested Alcinous' decision. He was as a rock, shaken by no deadly fears. The oaths he had taken he would not break, and the Argonauts rejoiced. The Colchians perceived that if they did not accept his ruling he would close his harbor to their ships and trade, but they also bethought themselves of the wrath of Aetes should they return to Colchis without Medea. So they beseeched Alcinous to accept them in Phaecia as friends, and let them settle in that land; and it was done. Alcinous also invited Jason and Medea to remain in Drepane, but Jason shook his head.

"I have a mission to complete, and a throne in Thessaly to claim. And I have a father who is old and ill. If I am to see him again in this world, I must make haste."

When Alcinous and Arete perceived that Jason was determined to put again to sea, they gave to him and Medea many splendid gifts. And Arete also gave Medea, from her own attendants, twelve Phaecian maids to wait upon her in her new life in a foreign land.

Seven days they lingered in Drepane, and Jason and Medea dwelt in the Cave of Macris and ate figs and honey. On the seventh day the moon changed, and Zeus sent a fresh breeze with the dawn. The Minyae raised the great sail and boarded their gallant ship, and she sped before the wind.

Through the Ambracian Gulf, past the land of the Curetes and the narrow islands of the Echinades they skimmed with sail spread wide. The salt spray flew, and Medea in the stern by Jason stood proudly in the blazing sun. Jason lifted a bronzed arm and pointed.

"See there, to the left? That is the land of Pelops. Around it and through the islands, and but a few days' journey and we reach my home." There was a boyish eagerness to his voice that Medea had never heard, and her heart was touched. Then he straightened, sniffing the air sharply, and his tone changed.

"The wind has shifted. A storm is coming from the north across the Peloponnese!"

Like an eagle swooping down upon its prey, the storm engulfed them. Lowering clouds scudded across a slatelike sky, and the sun hid its face. Then the rains came, beating like arrows upon storm-tossed *Argo,* and the men crouched beside the rowing benches and took shelter beneath their battle-shields. The young maids of Medea clung together, weeping like twittering sparrows. For nine days and nine nights the gale winds swept the ship south across the Libyan Sea. Medea, sheltered beneath her husband's cloak, lifted her face to the storm and wondered if it was the curse of Zeus.

Steadily the skies grew darker, and on the ninth night the blackness closed in thick and impalpable. Ancaeus, laboring vainly at the helm, cried out his grim despair. "Shoals are everywhere, and seaweed like tangled fingers from the deep, reaching out to draw us down to the mouth of Hades. The far reaches of my mind tell me where we must be. We are in the gulf of Syrtis, from which no ships escape. There is no help, no exit, no living creature on ground or in the air. Only the waters, and the spindrift blowing, and beyond, sand, to the dim horizon. As for myself, I think we are in the hands of the spirits of the dead."

Or the wrath of Hecate. A tremor shook Medea's soul. If it were so, then it was she who had brought this fate to Jason and his crew. Better far a valiant death on the field of the earthborn men, than to perish like this, unnamed and never known. She tried, but could not pray.

The swell of the sea lifted *Argo* high and drove her into the unknown dark. She rose, and groaned, and tilted backward, and men fell over themselves in terror and in fear. Then a wall came at the gallant ship out of the blackness, seizing her, holding her. Only the rain beat down, and the waves around her stern, but she did not move, and the wind made formless moan around her keel.

Dawn came only as a cessation of blackness and of rain.

Those aboard *Argo* lifted themselves to gaze blankly upon a lifeless world. The tide, racing in across a broad beach, had flung *Argo* on the inner shore, her keel dry and high. Now the tide had gone. A landscape, insubstantial as the mist around them, stretched away, unbroken. No paths, no watering place, no distant farm. Silence reigned over a silent world.

"Better we had dared again the Clashing Rocks against the will of Zeus," Jason said bitterly. "We might have perished, but we would have aimed at glory." He swung himself down over the side of the beached ship, and Medea followed to stand beside him on the sand, already drying in the heat. How could they survive here, even the fewest days? She looked with horror at the desert spreading out before them as the mist dissolved.

Ancaeus the helmsman, who had been their guide since Tiphys died, could not conceal his grief. "There is no way out. We are bound here in this desolate land. I have looked round, as far as I can see. Everywhere are shoals, and the great waves rolled in across the endless sand. Long since would *Argo* have been smashed to bits, had not a flood tide swept her in from the deep sea. Now the tide ebbs, and there is nothing left, only light surf that scarcely wets the ground. No ship could sail it, even if an offshore wind should come. We must abandon hope. If someone else feels the urge to try, let him take the helm and show what he can do. As for me, I do not believe Zeus intends to let us see again the shores of home." Unmanned by disaster, he sat down and wept.

In silence the Argonauts crept down from beach-bound *Argo,* and their cheeks grew pale. In twos and threes they began to wander ghostlike, as men do in some doomed city when the statues of the gods are sweating blood. And their feet dragged in the endless sand.

When night came, they embraced one another in tears and silence and went apart, as animals by instinct seek a place to die alone. They spread out, bypassing one another, and wrapped their heads in their cloaks and lay down without food or drink on the cruel sand. Medea's little maids, younger even than she, gathered round their stranger mistress and laid their gold hair in the dust. All the long night their pitiful lament, like the twittering of unfledged birds, rose to the merciless heaven. But Jason went apart, alone, and Medea's heart went with him.

The endless night ended in a hopeless dawn, and no man stirred. All throats were parched, and all tongues grew thick. Each man huddled under his own cloak, waiting for death and dreaming his separate dreams. As the high sun scorched the burning earth, came thick-crowding fancies, and to Medea's ears the moaning of her maids seemed like the song of the dying swan. Yet her thoughts were all on Jason. She threw her mind to weave a filament of dreams, all the days and years of the life together they were not to have. She saw them young and joyful, entering the foreign city that was his home. She saw them in their prime and pride, ruling in time over Iolcus as queen and king; saw them with children thronging happily about their knees; saw them together in the dignity of age, loved and respected by their kingdom and their land. Summoning all her powers, she went deeper and deeper into the vision, out of reach of the burning sun. And the sun reached the height of noon.

Then it was that a cry rang out across the scorching sands, a cry of hope and determination, like the roar of a lion calling across the jungle for his mate. At first she thought it was the cry of her own visions. Then, as she pushed back her sweat-stained veil, she beheld Jason, silhouetted black against the blazing sun.

Like a lion he stood, or like the image of a god, tall against the white sky with the sand and dust clinging to his black-bronzed skin. And he called them together, bidding them sit down in the patch of shade that was thrown by *Argo*'s shadow.

"Listen, my friends!" Jason's voice rang in the shimmering heat. "To me in my distress of death has come a vision. As I waited, as you, for an unspeakable fate, three young maidens in goatskin capes removed the cloak from around my head. And they said to me, 'Why this despair? You are the men who fetched the Golden Fleece! You have roamed the world and done heroic deeds. Drive out your own despondency and rouse your men. When Amphitrite, Poseidon's loving wife, has unyoked the horses from his chariot, you must repay your mother for her sufferings all the long days she has carried you in her womb. If this you do, you will yet see again the sacred Achaean land. This they said, but before I could ask the meaning of the prophecy, they vanished. One moment they were there; the next, a mist had come between us, and they were no more."

The Minyae heard and were amazed. As they pondered in the silence, another vision formed, which all could see. In the flashing colors of the blazing sun, a great horse with a golden mane came bounding from the sea. He shook himself, tossing off showers of spray, then like the wind he galloped off along the shore.

Peleus leaped to his feet, overcome by joy. "Clearly, Amphitrite has just unyoked Poseidon's team. Hear me, friends! Who is our mother but the ship herself? For many months, *Argo* has carried us in her womb, and we have heard her groan in pain. Now let us carry her. Let us lift her to our shoulders and carry her across the wasteland in the path of the galloping horse. I feel sure he will not vanish inland but will lead us to some bay of deep sea water." All who heard felt that none could have interpreted the portent better, and they cast off fear.

Jason it was who first stood to face the others. "Let us do this thing at once. Though the way is long and hard, what lengths and hardships has mother *Argo* not seen us through? Let us then set out, and continue on, whatever comes, never resting, never tiring, but trusting in whatever gods there be to see us through." And he stripped off his excess garments, rolling his cloak into a pad, preparing to lift the hull of *Argo* on his sunburned shoulder.

Medea looked at him standing there, weary, haggard and determined. She brushed back a strand of salt-stiff hair that had fallen in her eyes. He looked not like the golden youth who had dazzled her from her balcony. Nor, either, like the god who had first touched her in a meadow drunk with flowers. The journey's hardships had aged him early, and the blind confidence of youth was gone. It was a man who stood there, neither boy nor god.

Perhaps it was, in part, that the scales had fallen from her eyes. Medea smiled, remembering how she had thought herself a woman because of the awakening passion raging in her veins. She had not known then that maturity was no more a thing of passions than it was of years.

"I know him now," she thought. It was a knowing that had nothing to do with the Cave of Macris. She had seen him as she had seen herself, in strength and weakness, flaws and secret fears. And, seeing, she still loved, loved without illusion.

She pulled off her veil, and the jewels she had put on to die as befits a princess, and rose to stand by Jason.

Together, with no aid but their own faith and strength, the Minyae lifted *Argo* to their shoulders. In pain and misery beyond all telling, they carried her cheerfully nine days and nights across the desert dunes. The sun blazed, and thirst burned within them, yet they continued on. Medea walked at Jason's side, and it was she who carried his battle armor across the scorching sands.

On the tenth day they came to journey's end, and set *Argo* down into the waters of the Tritonian lagoon.

IMAGES
OF DEATH

THEIR FIRST THOUGHT was to quench their burning thirst. Like mad dogs they dashed in search of fresh water, and almost at once to their dazzled eyes appeared what seemed a group of maidens. But as the whole company approached, the forms dissolved and turned to dust. To Orpheus, it seemed the hand of heaven was in this, and he stepped forth and prayed beneath the blazing sky.

"Blessed Powers, whether nymphs or spirits, of Olympus or the Underworld, we beg of you, lead us to water, springing from rock or ground, that we may slake this never-ending thirst. If ever again we reach our homes, we will honor you among the greatest gods, with gifts of wine and offerings at feasts."

A sob broke from Orpheus as he prayed, and the light shifted, and before their sun-dazed eyes a miracle occurred. What had seemed sand was grass; as they moved forward, shoots appeared, and beyond the next rise a hollow of saplings, poplar, elm and willow. The leaves whispered to them like voices of gentle nymphs. Beyond, the land rose from a base of rock, and from a cleft therein gushed water in a healing stream. The Minyae swarmed upon it like burrrowing ants. Refreshed at last, they rose with clear water still dripping from their sunburned faces. And now Jason saw what had not been seen before, the great body of a giant serpent half-hidden in the grass.

Only the tip of the monster's tail still twitched; the whole length of his dark spine showed no other sign of life. From the thick skin protruded poisoned arrows of curious design, and dying flies clustered in the festering wounds. The Minyae gathered round and wondered.

"There is only one man capable of this deed," said Jason slowly, "and indeed the pattern of these arrows proves it to be true. This must be the Garden of the Hesperides, and he who sought the golden apples has been here. Hercules, our friend."

The Argonauts, rejoicing, agreed this must be true, marveling at the strange chance that had brought the lost giant so near a short space before. The suggestion came at once: "Let those of us most fitted spread out across the sands and try to find him as he trudges off." Quickly it was done; the sons of the North Wind with their winged legs, nimble-footed Euphemus, and Lynceus of the long vision each set forth in different directions with his special skill. Canthus the noble also went, for he hoped to learn from Hercules the fate of old Polyphemus, who had been his friend.

Alas for Canthus, in his searching he came upon a flock of grazing sheep. At once the thought came to him of his famished comrades, and as he was attempting to drive the flock off towards their camp, the shepherd appeared and killed him with a true-flung stone. Lynceus, returning to *Argo,* having seen only the shadow of a lonely figure far across the distant sands, found Canthus' body. He ran and told the others, including Euphemus of the swift feet and the sons of Boreas, who had also unsuccessfully returned. All the Minyae were filled with anger for their fallen comrade. They rose, took their swords, and went in search of the shepherd named Caphaurus. They killed him, to avenge the death of Canthus, and then they took the sheep.

They took with them also the body of Canthus, that they might bewail and bury it with proper rites. It was as they were bearing it back to camp that another tragedy occurred. A snake, sluggish with heat and having no wish to harm unless harm was done it, lay sheltering in the sand. Mopsus, unseeing, brought the sole of his left foot down on the tip of the creature's tail, and the snake, in pain, coiled round his shin and bit his calf. Medea, who saw it happen, shrank back and cried out in sympathy and horror.

"It is nothing, Lady." Bravely Mopsus pressed his hand on the bleeding wound. Yet even as he did so, the numbness of the dark poison began creeping through him, and a mist began to form before his eyes. He sank to the ground, held in Medea's arms, as the snake in terror swiftly slipped away. By the time Jason and his friends raced up, Mopsus was already cold.

Medea rose. "You must not wait. We must bury him at once."

Jason roused himself and shook his head. "We will bear him back to camp and give him funeral rites with his companion."

"You do not understand. You do not know the way of snakes, as I do." Medea pointed, and the men recoiled. Already the poison venom was beginning to rot Mopsus' flesh; his hair had begun to fall from his mouldering scalp. Swiftly, with bronze mattocks, his sorrowing friends dug a grave both wide and deep. They pushed the body into it, and Canthus with him, giving them as solemn burial as they could. Then they returned to *Argo,* donned full armor, and went back in the burning sun to march three times around the grave and raise a mound above it.

The next morn a south wind blew and they embarked, hoping to find passage out of the Tritonian Lagoon. But since they knew no route, they drifted helplessly all the day, and the path of *Argo,* nosing round for outlet, was as twisted as the route of a snake wriggling for shelter from the scorching sun.

Orpheus turned to Jason. "Why do we not put to shore and offer a gift to the gods of this foreign land? They might be induced to help us on our way." They did so, and almost at once a young man appeared striding towards them. He held in his hand a clod of earth, which he stretched out to them by way of welcome.

"Friends, accept this gift. At present I have no better one to offer. But if you strangers, like many foreigners, have lost your way, I will be your guide across the Libyan Sea. I am Eurypylus, king of this shore, and I know its secrets."

Gladly Euphemus held out his hand to accept the clod. "My lord, we beg you, tell us anything you know of the Minoan Sea and the Peloponnesus, for that is our goal. We were driven ashore on your land by a heavy gale. We have carried our weighty ship across the sands till we came to this lagoon. Now we have no idea how to get from it to the land of Pelops."

Eurypylus stretched out his hand and pointed to the distant sea. "There is the outlet. The smooth dark water marks the deepest spot, but the fairway is narrow between the beaches where the breakers foam. Beyond, the misty sea stretches out to the land of Pelops on the other side of Crete. When you have reached open waters, keep land to your right and hug the coast as long as it runs north. When it angles towards you and then falls away, you may leave it at its projecting point and sail straight on. The work may be heavy, but do not be distressed. A happy voyage to you!"

Thus encouraged, the Argonauts set forth at once. They were determined to escape from the lagoon by their own rowing, and the oars moved sweetly in their willing hands. Behind them they saw the young king walk into the water and disappear from sight, and their hearts were warmed, feeling that one of the blessed ones had come to bring them luck. At his comrades' urging, Jason hastily selected one of the finest sheep, held it over the stern and sacrificed it, praying, "God of the Sea, you who have appeared to us, whoever you may be, graciously grant us the happy return we all desire."

He cut the victim's throat and threw the carcass into the water before the stern. In a moment they beheld in the sweeping foam the form of Triton the water god, guiding them towards the open sea, and the Argonauts cried out in awe at the wondrous sight.

So they reached the open sea and spent a day on shore. With the next dawn they raised the sail and sped before the wind. The following morn they sighted a headland, and a corner of wide misty sea beyond the jutting cape. Here the west wind died, and a south breeze sprang, sending the white clouds scudding. When the sun sank, and the evening star appeared, the south wind failed, and they furled their sail and lowered the tall mast. All that night they rowed hard at the polished pinewood oars, and all through the next day and through the following night. They were still far from land when the high rocks of Carpathus greeted their sight.

"We shall sail," the helmsman Ancaeus decided, "across the stretch of sea to the great isle of Crete, and there seek shelter." And so they did. The day was now far spent, and the Argonauts were exhausted from their labors and their sleepless nights. Longingly they thought of shore and haven, yet just as they entered into Dicte's harbor and were preparing to make fast, a fearsome threat appeared. Jason, who saw it first, had scarcely time to shout a warning.

"Rocks! Look out!"

A giant boulder, larger than a man, crashed from the mountaintop into the sea beside them and barely missed the stern. The Minyae, who were tying tight the ropes, fell back in panic. Another rock crashed near, and yet another.

"Back water!" Ancaeus shouted above the flying spray. Not waiting for his comrades' clumsy fingers, he seized a knife and slashed the ropes that held them fast, and they hastily rowed away. Safe out of reach, they peered through foam and gathering dark and upon the rock cliff saw a form that chilled them through.

Some force of nature, god or human? They did not know; to their terrified, exhausted eyes it seemed a monstrous figure, formed like a man, but with skin of bronze. Many cubits tall it stood. Its mighty feet straddled the inlet up which they hoped to sail, and ever and again from its upraised arms crashed down gigantic rocks to bar their way.

"There is no help for it. We must sail on." Ancaeus rubbed his weary arm across his eyes and gave the order for the ship to turn. The aching men, faint with thirst, bent to the oars.

"Wait! You must listen!" Medea pulled herself up, willing strength to her own parched voice. "It may be I, I only, can defeat this man. You know I have some powers. Wait, keep *Argo* out of range of the rocks, and let me see if I can bring him down."

They did as she requested, resting their arms upon their oars and waiting to see what witchly power this frail woman could employ.

Medea wrapped herself in her purple mantle, pulling it high so that it veiled her face, all but her eyes. She reached out her hand for Jason, and he led her across the benches, past the Argonauts' curious, speculative eyes. Alone in the prow, she closed her eyes and began her incantations, invoking the spirits of the dead and the hounds of Hades, those fierce messengers of Hecate who feed on souls and haunt the lower air. She sank to her knees upon the sea-wet deck and called upon them thrice in song and thrice in spoken prayers. And the men waited, and the rocks yet crashed.

Finally she opened her eyes and peered off through the misty air. The dying sun glinted on the motionless figure of gleaming bronze. Behind her, on the pitching ship, she heard a faint trace of laughter, quickly hushed. There remained yet another form of power, which she knew but had never tried. Though her heart quailed, Medea closed her eyes again and steeled herself with all the malevolence at her command, summoning up from the dim reaches of her mind dark images of death. When her slight body trembled with malignant evil, she opened her eyes and fixed them across the separating sea directly on the eyes of the bronze giant. And the force of her thoughts went from her, in that glance, and entered into his. In an ecstasy of shuddering rage she filled her brain with visions of destruction, and their annihilating power crept like poison into the reaches of her adversary's mind.

Medea held her breath, her bloodless fingers gripping *Argo*'s rail to hold herself erect as the strength drained from her. But still her eyes remained fixed with their debilitating beams. Slowly, slowly, the crash of rocks diminished, the movements of the giant became clumsy. Then at last, as he lifted a heavy rock above his head, he stepped back without caution. His ankle, the one spot on his body not of protective bronze, was gashed upon a knife-sharp point of stone; blood gushed out like a wine-dark fountain, draining away his life.

For some moments the figure stood motionless, high on the jutting cliff. Then, faintly, the form began to sway. Forward, backward, forward, farther and farther, and then came down, like a tall pine, with a resounding crash.

The Argonauts spent that night, at last, upon the shore of Crete. By dawn's first light the men raised up a shrine to Athene, goddess of the island, and worshipped there. And Medea went apart alone into the forest, spent, and offered thanks to her dark goddess who had not returned desertion for desertion.

After filling their water jars, they again embarked, intending to row that day round Cape Salmonium. By night they were well out into the wide Cretan Sea. And there fear fell upon them, for they had entered what sailors know of as the Pall of Doom. It was a night of Hecate, and no star shone. No beam of moonlight pierced the thick engulfing dark. Chaos had descended, though whether from sky or up from the abyss of Hades they could not tell. Indeed, in terror, they half-wondered whether they had stumbled from wholesome seas into the dark rivers of the Underworld. All they could do was commit *Argo* to her mother sea, and drift where the sea would will.

Jason stood, at his seat beside Medea, and he lifted up his arms to the dark sky, weeping as he prayed. "Phoebus Apollo, god of light and manhood, I call upon you. Save us, your servants, who have wandered storm-tossed across the waters of the earth. And I will give you gifts in Pytho, gifts in Amyclae, gifts in Ortygia, gifts innumerable." And the tears ran down the weatherbeaten cheeks of the man, who long before, at journey's starting, would have scorned tears as unmanly, scorned the thought of help coming from invisible gods.

Beside him, Medea caught her breath and touched his arm. "Look, beloved!"

Argo had drifted round a curve, and before them through the darkness, came beams of dazzling light. The beams illumined a small islet, one of the Sporades, and with thankful hearts the Minyae brought their ship to harbor.

In a few short hours dawn came to show them the isle on which they had landed, and they called it Anaphe, or Revelation, since Apollo had revealed it to them in the night. There in the shelter of low trees they consecrated ground and raised an altar to Apollo, Lord of Light. Since their stores were few, they had little left to offer, only water for libations on the burning logs. And the little maids of Medea, accustomed to Alcinous' rich sacrifices, were amused. The men, too, after an indignant moment, laughed. Soon, lighthearted with exhaustion, they were all frolicking on the beach.

Their journey now was almost at an end, and fair seas beckoned and their cares departed. With the next clear dawn, they cast their hawsers off and sailed into the path of the golden sun. Jason went to Medea, standing in the stern, and flung his arm around her shoulder, his spirits high. "Soon now! Soon you will see the gold-touched pillars of my homeland, and the city of proud horsemen that I will rule!"

Euphemus, the swift runner, came up beside them, holding

in his hand the clod of earth the god-man they had met in
Libya had given him. "I dreamed a dream of this last night,"
he said. "I dreamed I held it to my breast and suckled it with
milk. But as I did so, it turned into a virgin maiden more than
passing fair." He flushed and grinned ruefully. "In the dream
I, being human, took her and lay with her. And then I felt re-
morse, but she consoled me, saying she was no mortal maid, but
of Triton's stock and nurse of my children yet unborn. She bid
me give her a home in the sea, near Anaphe's isle, and she
would reappear in the light of day to welcome my children's
children."

Jason, uttering an exclamation, clapped him on the back.
"My friend, you are marked for great renown! Cast now this
clod of Libyan earth into the sea, and the gods will make an
island of it. For it was Triton, and none other, who met us on
the Libyan desert, and who gave you this!"

Euphemus' heart was filled with joy, and at once he hurled
the clod into the sea. And Medea turned towards him, her voice
filled with a strange light. "Hear me also, high-hearted man
and son of the ocean god, for I too am prophet. You shall lie
with foreign women and beget a chosen race, which shall come
to this island and be lords of the dark-clouded plains. And from
the wave-beaten land shall go a stock that shall beteem the land
of Libya, and cities shall rise, and the world shall know of it.
Your children shall drive swift horses, and stormfoot chariots."

Medea's words dazzled her hearers' ears, and the Minyae
were silent, listening to her deep wisdom.

Swiftly now *Argo* sailed over great stretches of the rolling
sea and put in presently at the harbor of Aegina. They were
again short of water, but they wished to waste no time since
the wind held high, so they turned the gathering of water into
a game, and raced one another back and forth from spring to
ship. Then, refreshed, their spirits high, they sailed again across
the gentle sea. And Ancaeus, with a joyful heart, announced,
"We steer, from now, direct towards Pagasae!"

STRANGERS
IN A
STRANGE
LAND

IV

RETURN
TO IOLCUS

A S THE SHIP CLOVE the waters, the thoughts of
Jason grew somber for his mind returned to Aeson.
He stood in the prow, gazing out across the quiet sea,
wondering what welcome awaited him in Iolcus.

Medea sat on the polished rowing bench, watching the still
figure. She sensed his distance and divined his thoughts. Presently she went to him, putting her arms around his muscled
shoulders and leaning her head against his breeze-whipped
cloak. "Your sorrows are my sorrows, and your troubles mine.
Why does my husband grieve at thoughts of home?"

Jason did not turn, his eyes squinting against the sun towards
the far horizon. "It has been many months. At first I dreamed
of a hero's welcome in the public square. But much has happened. Now I think of an old man in a quiet room. Only my
mind sees visions of an empty house and a dead hearth. My
father was sick and aged when I left."

Medea's thoughts flew backward to Colchis' dark forests and
the rites of Hecate. Hecate, goddess of the lands of the dead,
whose power she, Medea, had once possessed. Her hands tight-

189

ened on Jason's shoulders and her whisper was a vow within his ear. "It is now near the night of the full moon. Set me ashore on some deserted forest before we reach your homeland and it may be I yet have some power to bring your father back his youth."

She went apart from Jason and brought forth her bronze-bound chest. Opening it in secret, she counted over its contents, then shut her eyes tight against the white Aegean sun and bid her mind remember. Jason watched, but did not come near her, though he spoke to the helmsman Ancaeus. And on the night when the full moon shone, they put to shore.

The night was still, and no breath stirred. The stones of the beach shone silver in the moonlight, and beyond them, past a motionless field, the thick-clustered forest was a yawning dark. Medea, stepping barefoot through the lapping waters, turned to Jason and grasped his hands. She had put on a black robe, and the strange light made her slender fingers look like claws of gold. "Stay here as you have promised, and do the things I bid you. You must not follow after me, whatever comes!" She turned and walked across the empty shore until her small figure was swallowed up by night.

Alone in the still field, she flung herself prone upon the living ground and prayed to the stars and moon, to all other powers of nature, and to the unknown gods of this alien land. She prayed to Hecate, for absolution and for aid, and her tears fell like burning rain, and overhead the stars shone brighter than they had done before.

For nine nights she kept herself from Jason's bed, spending the hours from dusk to dawn in fields and forest, seeking potent plants and herbs. She raised two altars, one to Hecate, and one to Hebe, goddess of youth. Then, on the night when the moon and stars were right, Jason and his companions brought ashore a ram as black as pitch. They did not stay, but left him standing docile on the shore while they withdrew that the ritual might not be defiled by eyes profane.

Out of the forest, after they had gone, Medea came. Her arms were bare in the starlight and adorned with oddly wrought bracelets and curious jewels, and her hair streamed like black flames upon her shoulders. Between the two altars she sacrificed the sheep, slitting its throat with the blade that had killed the prince of Colchis, and catching in a bronze bowl the dripping blood. She poured libations of milk and honey upon the altars, and she prayed to Hades and Persephone, rulers of the dead, that she be allowed to keep Aeson longer outside the gates of their darksome realm.

Thrice she circled the altars, murmuring her secret rites; and from the blaze she drew flaming twigs, which she dipped in blood and returned again to the fire to be consumed. And the fire leaped high, she felt the ancient savage power stirring and surging alive again within her veins.

It was time to prepare the sacred cauldron. She opened reverently her bronze-bound chest and the bundle of her cloak, which contained the things she had gathered in the woods by night. One by one she fed the cauldron, like some great beast, the ingredients of the charm.

I give thee stones of the East, which I have carried over
  many mountains, and over dangerous seas.
I give thee sand from all-surrounding Ocean, father of us all.
I give thee hoarfrost, gathered by light of moon.
I give thee countless things without a name.
I give thee all these things for the life of Aeson!

In the cauldron the myriad things boiled and seethed, and Medea stirred the brew with an olive branch, and saw it send forth green shoots and felt it quicken in her hand like a living thing.

When the spell was done, she put out the altar fires, took apart the altars, and returned all things as they had been before. She poured the potion into an urn she had prepared, and cleansed the cauldron with fresh water from a running stream.

Then she wrapped around herself the midnight cloak and came out of the woods to Jason.

She saw him waiting for her in *Argo*'s prow, not looking inland in violation of his vow but gazing out across the endless sea. She knew again, as she had known in Libya, that already age had touched him. Her own skin, unaccustomed to this southern heat, felt taut across her cheekbones, and for a moment she felt the chill breath of Hades on her neck. She picked up the cauldron, the urn and precious chest, and walked straight across the shifting stones toward her beloved. In the morning they sailed again towards Iolcus.

The sun shone bright as they neared the familiar shore. Now the coast of Attica appeared to their left side, and they sailed easily past Euboea and Aulis and the cities of Opuntian Locris. The rocky flanks of Pelion came to view, and the high ground where stood the cave of Chiron. Jason strained his eyes, but no figures could he see.

Medea came to stand beside him, linking her arm through his. "Soon, beloved! Soon we shall reach the shores of Pagasae and all the city will ring with the deeds of the hero Jason!" He did not respond, but his hand tightened over hers.

In honor of her husband, Medea had put on her golden gown, and the curious crown with shimmering jewels. Jason too had donned his splendid armor, and the helmet with the purple crest, and the richly embroidered cloak. Together they stood, watching the nearing shore, while around them sounded the joyous cries of the Minyae lords as they recognized the sights of home.

At last they neared the sands of Magnesian Pagasae and ran *Argo* ashore on the familiar beach, fastening the binding ropes for the last time. The sun stood high in the sky, bleaching the burning rocks, but no figures moved, no welcoming crowd appeared over the crest of the nearby hill. Jason scanned the inland horizon, peering off through the distance along the dusty road to Iolcus.

"We must decide whether to march bodily into Iolcus now, or wait until tomorrow for Pelias and his nobles to discover we have come."

Behind him on *Argo*'s deck, no excited discussion spurred. The journey was over, the men who had been bound so closely together through trials and triumphs were longing for their own separate hearthsides and were eager to be gone. The quest for the Golden Fleece had been the adventure of them all; the return of the Fleece to Iolcus and the claiming of Pelias' promise was Jason's dream alone. Already Admetus, king of Pherae, the Arcadian contingent, and the twins from Sparta were packing their prizes and their battle gear, gripping the other Argonauts' arms in gestures of farewell. Soon only Acastus, son of Pelias, and a few others from the Thessalian land were left with Jason and Medea and the sons of Phrixus to turn towards Iolcus in the sun of afternoon.

Jason squinted towards the yellow inland dust, and his lips tightened. "The journey started as the dream of one man alone; so it shall end." He picked up his weapons and the great bundle that contained the Fleece, and swung them down over *Argo*'s side onto the pebbled beach. Then he jumped down himself and, turning, held out his arms to catch his wife. Spears in one hand, the heavy bundle on his other shoulder, he started up the road toward the promised city, and Medea walked beside him. Behind them came Acastus and the sons of Phrixus. They walked steadily up the rising path, following Jason's lead.

What were they thinking there, Medea wondered. What was her husband thinking? To Acastus this must be a difficult homecoming, for she knew he had defied the king to sail. For Argus and his brothers? They had been reared since infancy on tales of their father's golden land. As for herself, she knew only that she had come at last, in this unknown country, to journey's end.

She hurried to keep up with Jason's stride, troubled at his

taut lips and somber eyes. How terrible, if after all he had endured, his dreams proved dross.

The sun of Greece, whiter and hotter than in her homeland, beat down upon the heavy cloak and made a burning circlet of her crown. They were nearing the city now; the barren fields gave way to squat white houses. Here and there livestock grazed, and grapes and olives twisted grotesque fingers toward the cerulean sky. Now the road grew narrow; figures came, townspeople and peasants, intent upon their business. They gazed at Jason and passed on, incurious.

"This is not like Jason's first coming," Medea thought, for he had told her of that triumphant entrance, half-naked in leopard skin like a god. Now he wore the armor of the country and the people, accustomed no doubt to soldiers, were indifferent. It was at her they stared.

Gradually, as they approached the center square and crowds grew thicker, Medea grew more conscious of the whispers. She straightened, eyes narrowing to slits.

For the first time it was borne upon her what it meant to have become an alien in an alien land. Here, all the faces that they passed resembled Jason. Handsome or ugly, they blurred together into one, flat-cheeked, their eyes straight-set, their faces oddly colorless. Their garments too seemed colorless and shapeless, unlike hers. She felt, suddenly, like an exotic imprisoned bird.

Her head stayed high, but she pressed close to Jason. "Where are we now?"

"The Acropolis of Iolcus. There, up that road, is the palace of the king." Jason lifted his head and squinted off into the sun. Behind her, Medea heard a whisper spreading through the crowds. Down from the height where Jason pointed whirled a wicker carriage drawn by milk-white mules. At the reins, erect, stood an aging man with the face and talons of an eagle.

"My father comes," Acastus said to Jason.

Jason stiffened. Involuntarily his hand crept to the hilt of his tested sword, and Medea pressed close beside him. A cloud of dust rose, spattering them like sifted mist, as the carriage stopped and haughty old eyes inspected them up and down. Around them, the curious pressed in a respectful circle, and the whispers stilled.

"Who are you, vagabonds and mountebanks who enter our city unannounced with foreign trumpery to dazzle the eyes of fools?"

Jason's voice rang through the suddenly quiet square. "Jason, son of Aeson, returned from the end of the world with the trophy you demanded and to claim your throne!"

"*Boy!*" The old voice was heavy with contempt. "It would become you better to weigh your words with reason and make no idle threats. It may be you can take the throne when I am gone, if you can prove your right and back your claim by force. As for me and the people of this city, we are no such fools as to turn over crown and power for no reason to an upstart pretender and his foreign whore!"

Jason's mouth tightened, but his voice maintained its even calm. "You gave your word, before all people in the public square."

"Word! Words are for the weak. The strong do not need them. Fool and son of a fool, where are the men at arms to enforce your claim?" Deliberately, looking him up and down, the old king spat at Jason's feet.

The world was very still.

Jason's eyes blazed. With a swift imperious gesture he pulled from his shoulder the bundle he had brought. "Here is the coverlet you sought. Let us see how well it protects your crumbling bones from the winds of death!" And he spilled into the dust of the public street the matted glowing skeins of the Golden Fleece.

Round about him the murmur of the crowd rose in the sound of awe. Pelias jerked at the reins, swung the mules round, and galloped off towards the palace. Acastus his son went with him. Jason turned and gazed off down the road up which he'd come, towards the memory of *Argo*.

"Jason." It was another voice, quieter and weak. His uncle, Pheras, came limping up, reaching out gnarled hands, tears running from his age-filmed eyes. "Jason, my boy. It has been so long, and we all feared—This looks not like a welcome."

"Another welcome is missing. Uncle, where is my father Aeson?"

Silence. Then Pheras stretched his hand. "Come to my home, you and your party. Rest and have wine. Then we will speak of Aeson."

"We will speak now." Jason's voice sharpened. "I must know what has happened since I sailed from Iolcus."

"At first nothing. The people watched and waited. And they talked, and Pelias moved with caution. But months went by. People forget, Jason; it is a fact of life. Only Aeson had faith. Day after day the frail flame burned. And the days passed, and winter came, and Pelias was certain you would not return. Only the people still were reminded by the words of Aeson." The old voice broke. "When Pelias was sure *Argo* had met some foreign doom, he forced Aeson to drink the blood of a bull, which is a potent poison. Your mother Alcimede, half-mad with grief, burst that night into the palace before all the people. She put a curse on the house of Pelias, and then died by her own hand."

A pause. Jason stood as one turned to stone. The old man went on. "You are weary, and dumb with grief. Come to my house. Rest and eat, and then we will talk further."

Jason shook his head. "The others can go with you, Argus and the other sons of Phrixus. As for me, I will spend no night under a roof of Iolcus unless it be in the chamber of the king."

He turned, and strode unseeingly back towards the womb of *Argo*. And Medea his wife went with him. In her hand she held the precious flask prepared at Hecate's altar to restore the youth of Aeson. The flask which had been brought too late.

Jason, seeing it as he lifted her up over *Argo*'s side, laughed harshly. "Throw it away! Throw it into the water and let it make the old sea young! It is of no use now."

Perhaps not. But perhaps. . . . Medea, about to follow Jason's bitter order, stopped, her fingers tightening on the flask's thin neck. For a long time after Jason had gone below, she sat alone, gazing off into the dusty distance towards the Acropolis of Iolcus, thinking of children's love and of lost fathers. Her eyes narrowed, and her mind grew firm.

The pall of night fell upon the city, and when no light showed, Medea wrapped herself in the dark cloak stained with her brother's blood. She picked up her precious bronze-bound chest, and secretly she let herself down over *Argo*'s side. In silence and alone, she entered the guarded city, and by her magic she made all who beheld her see only an aged crone. Like a serpent descending on its prey, she glided on sandalled feet to the palace of the king. There she knocked, and when the door was opened she announced herself as an old woman with a message for the daughters of Pelias. And she was admitted to the women's quarters.

The daughters of Pelias crowded around her, expecting messages of love from besieging suitors. But she requested an audience alone, and when the servants all were gone she threw back her cloak, revealing herself as the foreign woman. The princesses were alarmed and would have cried for help, but she forestalled them.

"Do not call! I come not as a danger but to seek your help, for you are women, young as I, and like me royal daughters to a father whom you love. Pity me, who for passion has been stolen from the far edge of the world, to dwell among strangers far from my family's home. I would return to Colchis, to my father, where my husband would be honored as a prince among the people, as was Phrixus. But Jason will have none of it; he is possessed with the desire for Pelias' throne.

"His presence in Iolcus is a danger to you, too. How long

will a young man wait for an old man to die? If you will join me, I have devised a plan that will help us both. For I can work magic; I can make old men young." And she told them of the spell she had prepared for Aeson.

"For the father of Jason it is now too late. But not for your father, Pelias the king. I will use this elixir to give Pelias back his youth, if your love and courage are strong enough to stand the test. For look you, with Pelias young again, and virile, he will yet father many sons. He will live long, and many will be the heirs who will follow after him and contest with Jason for the throne of Iolcus. When Jason my husband sees Pelias restored to youth, he will abandon his futile dream and return with me to Colchis. And peace will be upon all our lands."

The daughters of Pelias were afraid, but they loved their father and longed, even as Jason, to see their parent again in splendid youth. Medea with wily skill played upon that longing. She opened her bronze-bound chest and burned many things upon the fire, and the sweet smoke dazed their senses. She ordered forth a cauldron, butchered an aged ram, and put the pieces with the contents of her flask above the flames. Soon she dazzled the eyes of the daughters of Pelias, for they saw issue forth from the cauldron a young lamb, which frisked and gambolled before he ran away. And they feared, and marveled, and believed.

And Medea laid before them the sacrificial knife.

"It must be done by you, for only those who are blood kin love enough to work this spell. At the coming hour midway between dusk and dawn, you must steal to your father's bed. You must cut his throat, and drink his blood, and you must cut up his body as priests do the sacrificial rams. Then bring to me the pieces, and I will pour my potion upon the bleeding wounds, and put them in the cauldron, and I will work my magic, and Pelias the king will step forth vigorous and young." Her eyes shot golden fire, and the princesses of Iolcus were bewitched.

They crept into their father's chamber, and when they saw him sleeping peacefully their spirits quailed. But out of their great love, they lifted up the sacrificial knife. Just as they laid it at his throat, Pelias awoke, and cried out his shock. Yet they steeled themselves and did what they had come to do. They butchered the body of the king their father. With his blood still wet upon their lips, they returned to Medea to have their dead made whole.

But Medea was gone. Only her laughter still reverberated in the empty room. And Jason, son of Aeson, was avenged.

THE LEGENDS
DIE

PELIAS WAS DEAD, but all went not as Jason had expected. The land of Iolcus did not rise up and cry for Jason. Memories are short when bloodshed threatens. The people did not remember Pelias as tyrant and usurper, or Jason as promised golden stranger and present hero. They knew only that the shadow of civil war fell on a land that had grown fat with peace, and that when such times come, however just the cause, it is the people of the land who suffer. They wanted only peace, to be able to shut their doors and have a little meat beside their fire.

Acastus, who had sailed with Jason, who had shared the trials and triumphs of *Argo*'s quest, Acastus who was also the first-born son of the murdered king, met with Jason alone behind barred doors in the silence of the night. None know what words were spoken. Some say Jason's cousin threatened him with instant death; some say Jason voluntarily turned over to Acastus the crown of Iolcus, content in the greatness of his heart with the knowledge that Aeson's fall had been avenged. Be that as it may, when weary dawn broke on the troubled city, the golden stranger and his dark woman were no more in Iolcus. The people hung the Golden Fleece in their city temple and forgot how it had come.

What is there to say, where is there to go, for heroes however young who have outlived their hour? Jason and Medea went to Corinth, for she herself had an ancestral claim to the Corinthian throne. They did not speak of that, however, to Corinth's king, referring only to a distant kinship. And the king of Corinth welcomed them, for Jason was the hero of all Hellas, and such men have in their time a kind of magic. Medea they accepted with wary eyes, noting her dark gold skin, her Colchian cheekbones, and her foreign jewels. And the hours and months of the years went hurtling by.

Only occasional small furies broke the pattern of the days. Jason participated in the Hunt for the Calydonian Bear, but the only wound he inflicted was a small one on himself. Once Aegeus, king of Athens, came to Corinth and while there, remembering *Argo,* paid a visit to the home of Jason. He was a good man, and he saw in the face of the dark woman the eyes of a young girl torn from her roots of home, and he was kind.

Medea knew her husband, and she knew when the athlete's golden body settled into the solidity of middle age, when the once taut muscles grew lax with easy living. She knew herself, too, and without recourse to mirrors of polished bronze could almost mark the moment when the witchery of adolescence gave way to the matronly set of a woman too early old. But still she wore the strange-toned, jewel-encrusted cloaks of Colchis, which were so alien to Grecian eyes, and wore them well, tall and proud at Jason's side. She let the murmurs of the populace eddy and swell and pass unnoticed in her wake like the voices of the wind.

Stranger, they called her. Alien. Foreigner. Seducer. Witch. The words fell around her and behind her like feathers from the wings of the birds of night. She set up a secret altar in her house and worshipped, with a sense of hopeless despair, her abandoned goddess. In time her body swelled with child and she was, irrevocably, a girl no more. But with the birth of her two sons, she found at last a modicum of peace. And if, in the dark watches of the night, she longed for a world that was gone, she did not speak.

BETRAYAL

JASON, THE GOLDEN HERO of the Fleece, was growing old, and the poets no longer sang his fame. He lived quietly in Corinth, and Medea also lived quietly, finding with irony that a woman who lives thus, withdrawn and to herself, gains as bad a reputation as those who are overproud. Foreigners, especially, must be adaptable, and to these Greeks she was and would remain a foreigner until the end of time.

"Why then adapt?" she thought with bitterness. "What use?" And she wore her foreign garments, foreign jewels with her head held high, and ran her house with its inner courts and double gates after the manner of the homes of Colchis. It became everything to her to think well of one man. And he, her husband, turned and betrayed that trust.

Creon the king of Corinth had no heir, only a daughter whom he greatly loved. Creusa, princess of Corinth, had golden hair, Grecian profile and a body just ripening into adolescence. She was just the age Medea had been when Jason first beheld her; and when his eyes fell on Creusa now, his blood stirred in his veins and his heart lusted, for she brought back his vanished youth and forgotten dreams. And Creon, remembering Jason's past renown, needing an heir, forgot the woes that had come to bygone Cadmus when he gave a loved daughter to be a hero's second wife. He offered Jason Creusa's hand in marriage, and offered too, upon his death, the throne of Corinth. In Jason the lust for power burned fiercer even than the longings for lost youth, stronger than sacred vows. Deserting his children, deserting the wife of the Cave of Macris, he vowed to take a royal bride into his bed. Love was diseased; hatred was everywhere. Good faith was gone, and no more in Greece remained a sense of shame.

The news came to Medea only after the thing was all but done.

Her women, who heard the rumors first, were afraid to tell her, for they feared her violent heart. But on the morning when the wedding feast took place, the news at last came to her, and she shut herself in her room and cried aloud.

"Gods of this foreign land, I call on you! Behold the return my husband gives me for my love! Witness how he treats the vows we made each other, our right hands clasped in eternal promise!" Medea twisted and moaned to herself, calling her father's name.

"Aetes, Colchis, my home, my brother . . . all betrayed. For what? The love of a man determined to dishonor me. Now, now I know what it is to have lost my home." And she wept again, wasting away in tears, and would not eat. She threw herself upon the bed she had shared with Jason and lay like stone. No more than a rock or the surging sea would she listen to her attendants' anxious words.

Troubled, they brought her young sons to her, but she could not bear to look on them, for she saw in their wondering countenances the face of Jason. They whimpered, puzzled and afraid, and the servants led them off, murmuring among themselves of the strange woman.

Medea heard them, but she paid no heed. She heard too, though she did not show it, when the children's tutor entered shortly to whisper to the nurse the rumor now flying in the morning streets: Creon intended to drive the half-breed children and their foreign mother from the land of Corinth. Medea, with fierce effort, willed the whisper from her mind.

I will believe nothing, nothing until I hear it from the lips of Jason. But Jason, the fearless, did not come near the house that had been his home. And all the house was as a house of death.

"Old ties give place to new. Is that a fact I have only just discovered?" Medea laughed bitterly. "So each man loves himself more than his neighbor. Some with good cause, others for what they get. Oh, gods, I wish, I wish that I could die!"

Her troubled children tried to comfort her, but she flung herself away. "I hate you, children of a hateful mother. I put a curse on you, and on your father. May this whole house crash about our feet!"

"Why turn on them, poor sparrows? Can they share their father's wickedness?" Their old nurse knelt to gather them in her arms, but she faced Medea firmly. She was aged and wrinkled, stubborn with conviction, and she brought to Medea's mind the memory of her nurse at home. In the faded eyes Medea read a kind of pity. "Lady, Lady, give not way to wrath. The tempers of the great are terrible, for used to having their own way they shift with dangerous speed from mood to mood. What is moderate is best for everyone."

Medea, her passion spent, rested her brow against the cool stone of the wall. If only lightning from heaven would split that head and ease her pain. What use had she now for life? She lifted her weary face towards the heavens and called upon the watching gods. "Behold the things I suffer, the promises forgotten. I pray that I may see my husband suffer. Him, and his bride, and all their palace. I ask it in the name of Zeus, Keeper of Oaths!"

She dropped her head against the wall, and the old nurse, in helpless pity, scuttled out and bid the servants play sweet music. But none of them had discovered a blessed tune to put an end to grief.

What an unfortunate thing it was to be a woman, Medea thought with wry despair. First she must buy a husband, and take a master to her body, for not to have one was even worse. Married, she was thrust headlong into new ways of life. If she had learned well from her mother the devious guile of manipulating the man who shared her bed, if he bore his yoke lightly, life could be good. If not, it could be a living death. How easily a man who was ignored at home could leave his house and find companionship with friends or other women, while custom demanded she keep her eyes on him alone. And she was told she had an easy life compared to his in the battlefield reality of the world.

A scornful laugh stirred within her. "I would rather stand three times in the front rank of a battle than bear one child." But that was something a man would not understand.

Perhaps it was different for some women, she thought restlessly. The ones secure and contented with a family at home, who enjoyed life and the company of friends. The ones—the traitorous thought welled up unbidden—who had married men wiser than they, who had not discovered the powers of their own minds. Not so she, Medea, princess, priestess, skilled in many arts, a refugee, now thought of by Jason as a pawn he had brought back from a foreign land. She had no longer parents, brother, anyone with whom she could take refuge in this sea of woe.

A sound not expected jarred through her reverie. The bronze gong that she had had made and hung by the courtyard's double gate, after the manner of her homeland, to signal the arrival of visitors. It seldom rang, for in this alien land she had few guests. She had no intimates, outside her household, where none were her equals.

Jason . . . it would be Jason, coming to meet her face at last, to speak the truth. Medea flung back from her ravaged face the hair that she had torn down in her grief. "Quickly—my paints, and the amber pins." Her maids, relieved to see her roused, scurried to obey. With shaking hands she lined her eyes with soot, stroked color on the lids, robed herself like a queen. Queenly, her steps regally slowed by the weight of her heavy cloak, she entered the outer court. But the face she beheld was not the face of Jason.

Creon, King of Corinth. Medea's eyes flashed golden fire. "What brings the king in person to do honor to my humble home? Is it to revel in the sorrow he was wrought? Or because the foreign woman is thought unworthy to enter the palace grounds?"

"On the contrary." Creon's voice was resonant and calm. He spoke as Aetes did in delicate negotiation, and her mind grew wary. "I come to you in recognition that you too are of royal blood. And far from thinking you inferior, I respect your powers. That is what brings me here. That, and your threats." He paused, while they measured each other like contending warriors before a single combat. "I have heard the words you have spoken against your lover and my daughter. I have come in person to order you to leave my land at once, you and your children. I have decreed it, and I will see it done."

Banishment. The word sank slowly through the levels of her mind with its multiplicity of implications. She wet her lips. "What is your reason, Creon, for ordering me to exile?"

"I fear you," Creon said bluntly. "There is no shame for a wise man in acknowledging a rightful fear. I love my daughter, and I fear for her. You are clever, and skilled in evil arts, and you are angry over losing Jason's love. I would rather bring your hatred on me, now, than be softhearted, and have my daughter pay."

Medea shook her head. "I tell you, Creon, I hope my children grow up like their father, rather than with their mother's mind. This is not the first time I have suffered for it. Cleverness makes its possessors objects of envy and ill-will. Those who put new ideas before the eyes of fools are themselves thought foolish, and those who are thought superior will end up hated." She looked at Creon with a weary laugh. "I do not hate you, Creon. And do you think that I, myself royal, would question the authority of a king? It is my husband who has incurred my hate. You have acted wisely, doing what seemed best for your daughter and your land. You wanted a mighty hero for your daughter, and Jason is the hero of the Fleece. He has done little since, but still a hero. Small matter that he is already married."

"Your liaison was no true marriage."

"It was a marriage!" Medea's voice flared. "In red and gold, consecrated by sacrifice and vowed before the gods." She stopped. "No, I do not blame you. And may your daughter have better luck in her love than I in mine. Only let me live in this land, and I will not raise my voice."

"When your words are gentle, I trust you less than I did before, for gentleness can be a mask for guile." Creon's voice was cold. Oh, he was clever himself, that one, and shrewd as Aetes. Medea's respect for him grew, and with it grew her panic. She flung herself to her knees, clinging to his hand.

"I beg you, by your daughter whom you love. Pity me, who for the sake of Greece have lost a father, a brother and a home."

"You will go. The thing is fixed, so save your tears. Woman, are you determined to create a scene?" Creon's lip was curling, and Medea checked herself sharply.

"I will go into exile. That is not what I seek. It is my children I think of, how they are to be fed and where they are to live. You, who have a child yourself, have pity on them. Let them remain in Corinth one more day."

Creon looked at her. "I am no tyrant. Showing mercy has often made me loser, and it may do so now. But you shall have your wish. I tell you, though, if the light of tomorrow's dawn finds you or your children within the boundaries of my land, you die."

He turned and left, followed by his attendants; and Medea stood, never breaking her iron control, until he was gone and the gates tight shut behind him. Then she swung round and went straight to her inner chamber, pulling the curtains closed. She drew the pins from the heavy weight of hair that made her head ache dully, and closed her eyes.

Life went so badly. As from a great distance she looked back upon herself as a girl in Colchis, and she almost laughed. Her world had seemed so radiant with promise then, and crowned with splendor. Now? A day ago she had thought no worse harm could come to her, but she had been wrong.

A day. She had a single day. She must set her mind upon it. Creon was wise, but like Aetes he had a fatal flaw, and in Creon's case the flaw was kindness. To Medea, hardened by suffering, compassion was a weakness. It had brought her to her present pass; it existed in others but to be exploited. The doting father had become so foolish, she thought contemptuously, that though he could have made her helpless by immediate exile, he had put all futures into her hand by giving her a single day.

"How could he have thought I would have fawned upon him, even spoken to him, unless to gain my ends? Before the sun sets I shall see my enemies dead." In the scalding salt tears of the past day's torment, all her wishes, all her longings had crystallized to this one desire. There remained but to choose the means.

She knew many ways of death. The pictures rose before her eyes, tempting her with exquisite fingers of revenge. To set a fire beneath the bridal bed. To sharpen a sword and thrust it to the heart. No; there was infinite satisfaction in a death that she could watch, but if she were caught stealing into the new home of Jason, she would die—and what was far worse, give her enemies cause to laugh. Better to choose the path in which she was most skilled, the subtle art of poisons.

So be it, then. Poison was said to be a woman's weapon. She was born a woman. "And women of necessity," Medea thought, "have become the cleverest of contrivers." Never would she, daughter of Aetes, descendant of the Sun, be mocked before a foreign people by the son of a dethroned king.

Medea whirled, her mind set like the keen blade of a sharp-honed knife, and went directly to the cupboard where she kept the bronze-bound chest.

There was a commotion behind her, and then her maids were bursting in. A little maid, half-mute with terror, like the one long ago in Colchis. "Lady, Lady...."

Footsteps in the courtyard, striding closer. She had only time to thrust the chest back and swing round, holding the covering curtain tight shut behind her back. Her eyes shot fire.

Across the room, silhouetted in the doorway of her private apartments, as though he still had the right to come there, they looked upon the face of Jason.

SANCTUARY

FOR A MOMENT time was suspended, like the breath of a frightened maid. Yet even in those seconds her devouring eyes took in many things. He had gone to paunch; she had forgotten that in her grief. No more an athlete. The girl would tire him out. He'd drunk too much. Keeping up with the younger men? Keep that up, Jason, and you yourself will fashion my revenge. She willed her mind to concentrate on that, steeling herself against the other emotions, unexpected, which came swiftly crowding.

Then Jason opened his mouth, and all else fled before her hatred. For his voice was cool, contemptuous; his eyes traveled up and down her as carelessly as a marketplace dilettante inspecting a female slave.

"This is not the first time I have noticed how irrational you become when in a temper. Medea, had you been as reasonable as any man, you might have lived in Corinth, even in this house, in comfort. No, you could not do that. You talk wildly for neighbors and slaves to hear, and earn your exile. Your words cannot hurt me; say what you like. But you might have considered before you talked against a king. Believe me, you are lucky that exile is your only punishment."

Medea looked at him, fighting back the impulse to spit upon his feet. She would not lower herself to that extent. Taking her silence for a kind of welcome, Jason strode in easily.

"Contrary to your thoughts, I have never been against you. I have even spoken to the king on your behalf, else your punishment might be death. In spite of your conduct, I have come here to make some provision for you, so you and the children will not be penniless. Even though you hate me, I think of you pleasantly."

He stood there in a patch of sunlight, gazing upon her in Olympian complacency, and Medea's wrath exploded.

"You coward! Coward, and less than a man! You, my worst enemy, come here to do me favors! This is more than over-confidence, my husband, though that you've often had. It is more than boldness, which you've often lacked. No, you suffer, Jason, from the worst of all human diseases. *Shamelessness.* I saved your life, and all your Greek shipmates know it. I lulled the snake to sleep that you might steal the Fleece. I betrayed my father and my country, and murdered my own brother. I wrought for Pelias a dreadful death. All this I did for you. And what is my reward? You leave my side and take another bride to bed."

How terrible things between man and woman have become, she thought, when the only weapon she had was that which was the death of love: the debt of gratitude. Medea shook her head, feeling an insane desire to laugh. "Had I given you no children, I might have understood. Princes need heirs. But we have two sons whom I well know you love. As it is, looking on you, I can only think the old gods have ceased to rule, and new standards risen, since you so dismiss the oaths you swore me. A distinguished husband I have indeed—for breaking promises!"

"I broke no promises," Jason responded hotly, and she saw with a stab of triumph that she had drawn blood beneath his armor of indifference. "I never swore to have you as my only wife. Are the Olympic gods less godly because they share their love and honor with many women? Nor have I cast you off. Did not your feminine emotion cloud your vision, you would see this second marriage is in the best interests of us all. But no, you women, all you are concerned with is love. If that goes well, you think the world is rosy; if not, you think even things in your own best interest are most hateful."

Medea made a swift gesture, and Jason caught her arm. "No! Hear me out. And believe one thing, it was not for any woman I made this royal marriage. When have I needed such contracts for mere pleasure?"

"For reputation, then! You are finding as you get on in years it is not respectable to have a foreign wife!"

Jason's eyes blazed, and for a moment she thought she would be struck. Instead he swung away, grinding his fist into his palm, and when he turned to her again, voice calm, Medea knew that for the first time ever they faced each other naked, without the armor of their self-delusions.

"All right then, you have said it. Remember, Medea, how we came to Corinth? Refugees. Strangers, both of us, in a strange land." For a moment she saw behind the bloodshot eyes the golden youth who had sailed home from Colchis aflame with such bright promise. "What luckier chance for an exile than to form alliance with the royal family of his new country, and inherit in time the throne? I have been poor before, unknown, possessed only of youth and the honor of my name. But as you say, as one gets on in years, one learns many things. I have learned that fame is as fleeting as the flowers in the victor's crown, and provides as well for a man's children after he is gone. When a man's wealth leaves, his friends do also, and bygone fame means nothing to new generations. By this state marriage, I and my children can live in comfort and in honor . . . which I might have shared with you, had not your folly deprived you of it. You have only yourself to blame."

"Aye, for being fool enough to fall in love with you!"

"There you have it," Jason said brutally, and she saw he had put on again the armor of self-delusion because he was too weak to stand without it. "All that you say you did for me—it was not my need that impelled it, but your own lust. I did not need your help. And I have given you far more than you gave to me. I took you from life among barbarians, at the far end of the earth. I brought you to Greece, to live among civilized men and enjoy a world ruled by law instead of superstition and brute force. And all Greeks consider you a clever woman. You sailed on glorious *Argo,* and were first wife of the hero of the Fleece. Who would have heard of you had you remained in Colchis? What honors would you have known?"

"Honor!" Medea spat the word. "I, too, Jason, have learned as I grew older. Honor is relative. Life teaches women to be more realistic than you heroes, and at times honor is a luxury we cannot afford. Where am I to go now, I and my children? Back to Colchis, which I betrayed, to the father whose son I murdered? Shall I seek refuge with Pelias' wretched daughters? For you I have caused my friends to hate me, made enemies of those who never gave me harm. Where should I turn?"

"I am sure your cleverness will think of something," Jason said indifferently. His eyes traveled over her in casual contempt. "I would advise you not to try to seduce another husband. You women of the East, it seems, age young."

For one stunned second the words struck at her. Then she was at his face, her nails like claws. He grabbed her wrists, jerking her arms away and down so that she screamed with pain. "I will overlook this, and say again I am prepared to give you money, or letters of introduction to some friends."

Rubbing her bruised arm, Medea drew herself to her full height and spat with deliberate precision in his face. "I shall never take a thing from you, I or my children. Go to your Grecian bride! Enjoy your wedding, if you can. You may regret it!"

With impotent fury Jason wiped his face with the corner of

his cloak. Then he wheeled and was gone, and she was again alone, her passion spent.

The day was now half gone, and nothing done. Quite suddenly she had to be out of that house of suffocating memories. She seized a cloak and fled into the street, muffling the dark wool around her head to shield her ravaged face from speculating eyes. Where she was going, she neither knew nor cared, save that it was away from the close city, out to the healing forest, where she could draw strength again from the primal earth.

There were few people in the streets at the midday hour. No doubt those who had stirred from the coolness of their homes were round the palace, gathered like sheep to catch a glimpse of wedding splendor and Jason's royal bride. Medea walked swiftly, heedlessly, her eyes upon the dust of the road and her mind turned inward.

"Woman, can you tell me the way to the home of Jason of Thessaly?"

The voice came, close at hand, from nowhere, like the voice of a listening god. She looked up, startled, and the protective cloak fell back. The stranger, in his robes of dignity, drew back with a swift, shocked ejaculation.

"Forgive me, but are not you the Lady Medea, wife of Jason?"

Aegeus. The memory stirred in the numb recesses of Medea's brain. Aegeus the kindly, distinguished king of Athens who had paid a royal courtesy call on Jason during their first year in Corinth, when the halcyon days had not entirely fled. Aegeus the intelligent, who beneath alien clothes and skin had recognized her as his peer.

"That was my name," she responded with bitter rue. "Greetings to you, Aegeus. What brings you to this cursed country's soil?"

"I am returning from a visit to the oracle. My only son was lost to me some years since, and by some power of fate I produce no other heir. So I consult the gods." Aegeus shrugged wryly. "Phoebus replied in words too wise for mere man to guess their meaning. But what of you? What has happened to cause your grief?" He leaned closer, his wise eyes scanned her face, and she knew pretense was useless.

"He who was my husband has taken another wife."

Aegeus started. "Surely even Jason would not dare—"

"You may be sure he has."

"Has love dazed his senses? Is he tired of your great love?"

"Oh, he is greatly in love—with the idea of alliance with a king. Creon, who rules this land of Corinth, has given Jason his own ewe lamb as bride. And there is more. I have been banished, by order of the king." With a swift gesture Medea dropped to her knees in the dust by Aegeus' side. "My lord, I beg of you, take pity on me. It must be some gift of the gods that has brought you here. Receive me in your land, and at your hearth." Her frantic mind divined his hesitation. "I will end your childlessness and will bring blessings on you."

"For many reasons," Aegeus responded slowly, "I would like to help you. But it would not be prudent for me to provoke a quarrel with a brother king. I tell you this; I will lift no hand to help you out of Corinth. But if, of your own power, you can reach my house, you shall stay there safely. You can claim sanctuary, and to none will I give you up."

"It shall be so." Medea rose and grasped his arm, and her words came in a harsh whisper. "If I might have a pledge—"

Aegeus frowned. "Do you not trust me?"

"Aye, I do. But the house of Peleus hates me, and so does Creon. If they try to drag me from you, your oath will protect us both. If our pact is only words, you will be lightly armed. I am weak, while they have wealth and royalty to help them."

Aegeus nodded. "You have a mind that does become a queen. And you are wise. For me, an oath will be safer, and for you more certain. Name the gods by which you will have me swear."

"Swear by the Earth, and by the Sun, father of my father, and by all the gods, that you will never cast me from your land, nor in your lifetime hand me to my enemies."

And Aegeus swore, and they clasped right hands to seal the compact.

"I am satisfied! Farewell." Medea pulled the concealing cloak about her and turned back toward the city, a fierce exaltation burning within her. Now the die was cast. Zeus himself, and his daughter Justice, and her ancestor the Sun were witness. Now was the hour of her triumph over her enemies, however high the cost.

Medea set her feet firmly in the dust of the road to Corinth, and from that moment there was no turning back.

THE GIFTS
OF BLOOD

EDEA'S FIRST ACT, upon reaching again her home, was to send the old nurse hobbling after Jason. She was to find him at the palace, Medea said; she was to tell him her mistress had reconsidered, seeing now the royal wedding to be an excellent idea.

"Tell him," Medea said harshly, "to come to me at once, for I have matters of great import to tell him, and I would send a gift of friendship to the little bride."

And the old woman went, happy in her belief that things were going well. She would be some time, Medea knew, for the road was steep and twisted, and the old crone lame. And that was well, for there was much that she herself must do. She turned towards her own chamber, her heart at war within her.

She had at hand the means to best wound her husband, to make him pay the price—not with his own death, that could be too quick and merciful, but with living in years of pain. That it must make her, too, the unhappiest of women she knew; so it must be. No compromise was possible. Life held no profit for her anyway, for she had no land, no home, and there were none could give her children safety. Children by law were a father's property, to be raised or destroyed at will. Well, then, she would beg that the children not be banished but remain here under their father's care. He loved the children. She would humble herself, plead on her knees if need be.

"But in time . . ." Medea drew her breath with a stab of pain. "In time it will be seen that I am no weak woman, feeble-spirited, no stay-at-home. And I will be remembered."

She went into her private chamber, pulling the curtains tight behind her, and was closeted there alone for a long time.

The sun was already lowering in the sky when Jason came. He was in good spirits, wearing a splendid robe, obviously just risen from the wedding feast and full of his own graciousness in having done so.

"Woman, here I am at your request. Despite your bitterness, you see, I will listen to your wish."

Medea lowered her eyelids to hide their golden light. "I wish to ask your forgiveness," she said slowly. "I have been mad in setting myself against my husband and the king. My anger was foolish; I showed great lack of sense. Why, as your wife, I ought to have joined with you in this endeavor, which cannot but bring good fortune to our children." She called the children from the house, bidding them join hands with their mother and their father, who again were reconciled. And Jason, hearing what he wished to hear, believed.

"I approve your words," he said expansively. "Indeed, I cannot blame you for what you said before. It is natural for a woman to go wild when she is no longer her husband's only joy. But now you see truer, for you are, after all, a clever woman. It is too bad your wits return too late to prevent your banishment. But for our children, as you say, all will go well. I have made provision for them. I think in time to come they will be among the leading men in Corinth. Medea, why do you turn away, eyes wet with tears?"

"It is nothing. I was thinking of the children. Woman is a

frail thing, given to crying. Jason, as you love your sons, beg Creon that they may remain with you in Corinth. I fear for them, alone in a foreign land without a father's care."

Jason looked uncomfortable. "I will ask. I doubt he will agree."

"Then you must ask your wife to beg it from her father!"

"I will do it." Jason grinned. "I think with her it is safe to say I will succeed."

"Aye, you will, if she is like all other women! And I will help this, too; I will send her gifts. I give to her the gown which Helios the Sun bestowed on his descendants, and the diadem of the Children of the Sun."

Medea signaled to the servants and they brought forth from the house, on trays of bronze, the golden gown she had brought long before from Colchis and the little crown, its jewels shimmering in the light of the descending sun.

At the sight of them, Jason had the grace to look embarrassed. "Do not be foolish and give away your greatest treasures. There is no shortage of gowns within the palace, nor of gold for crowns. I warrant my bride considers I am already gift enough."

"Let me have my way! Gold does more with some than words. As for me, I would give not only gold, but my life itself, for my children's sake." And Medea turned and placed the trays of bronze in the children's arms.

"There, my sons. Go with your father and give these gifts from your own arms to the little bride. Beg her to let you stay with your father and not be banished. Go quickly, and return to bring your mother news."

And they went, with Jason, followed by their tutor who would see them safely home.

Medea stood in the little doorway and watched them go, her eyes like slanted slits. The trap was set. The little bride would accept the curse of gold, the grace and perfume and the glow of the splendid robe would work their spell upon her. Into the trap she would fall. And others with her.

Medea turned away blindly, her eyes welling up with sudden tears.

"Oh, I am lost, I am lost! The gods and I have contrived this in a kind of madness." She leaned her pale face against the door frame, and was still standing thus when the children and their tutor again returned.

"Mistress, I bring happy tidings. The children are reprieved. The royal bride condescended to take with her own hands the gifts you sent."

"How—did she take them? Tell me quickly."

The tutor smiled. "The hall was full of guests. And when we entered, the children following their father, all were astonished, and spoke of one thing only, how Jason and Medea had reconciled their quarrel. The princess' eyes were fixed eagerly on Jason. But when she saw the children her face grew pale, and she covered up her eyes and turned away."

So. She had been right, Medea thought, eyes narrowed. This young girl was no innocent pawn, but another Ino. "What happened then? Speak quickly!"

"Your husband sought at once to end the girl's bad temper, bidding her cease her anger and beg the king to let the children stay. She was not pleased. But then she saw the gifts, and she began to smile. Why, Lady, why this harsh sigh and bitter tears?" The tutor was a simple, kindly man, and puzzled. "Courage, Lady! You too will soon be brought home from exile by your children."

"Ah, before that happens, I shall bring others home." Medea straightened, willing her voice quiet and calm. "Go inside, and do for the children as it is your custom. I will come to them soon."

She turned her face away, not allowing herself to look upon them lest her purpose falter. *Oh, my children, you can have a city, you can have a home. Yet how can I leave you, aliens in an alien land? There is no safety for you, for the way is fixed. You have walked already along the path of blood.*

In her mind's eye she could see, as in a vision, the scene

within the palace, the skein of fate she had wrought beginning to unroll. Creusa the princess was young, imperiously impatient. She would be eager to put on the golden gown, would take the gorgeous robe and dress herself, with her own hands set the golden crown upon her golden hair.

Now she arranges the twisted curls before a shining mirror, now smiles at the lifeless image of herself, adoring. Now she rises from her chair and walks about, stepping softly with her little sandalled feet. Often and often she will stretch and turn, to see the gleaming gold. Soon now the color of her rosy face will change, and she will stagger, tremble and go pale. Barely will she reach the chair, and the white foam will break through her bloodless lips, and her eyes will roll. At first the servants will take it as an ecstatic fit sent by the gods. Then she will shriek, and they will run . . . to the fatuous king, to the new-wedded bridegroom drinking with his friends. The whole palace will ring with their shrieks and running. And she, poor fool, will be alone when she opens her shut eyes and comes to herself with a terrible groan of pain. . . .

As in her own flesh, Medea could feel the streams of all-devouring fire, the poisoned drugs in the golden tissue invading the pores of the unhappy girl's tender flesh. Soon, heated by her body, the potion would burst to flame. She would leap up and, running all on fire, try to shake from her hair the crown of gripping gold. Then more, and twice as fiercely, would the fire blaze out until, unrecognizable, she would fall down.

And now her wretched father would rush in. Neither the set of her unslanted eyes would he see, nor the shape of her flat-cheeked face. From her head would ooze out blood and fire, like pitch on pine bark, and her flesh would drop away. He would fall upon her, holding her in his arms, and like ivy on laurel the poisoned golden rags would stick to him, ripping the aging flesh from his stiffening bones. Her corpse would pull him close until his life was quenched.

Jason would not touch them. Jason cared too much for his

own skin to risk the danger, and that was good. Life would be more painful than oblivion.

The rays of the sun were sinking. She had little time. Her task was fixed; she must not hang back from the necessary horror; must not think. Afterwards, there would be a time for tears . . .

She called her children to her, and they came, excited and bewildered, happy to have back again their mother, this strange sad mother who held them tight and covered them with kisses so that they squirmed, embarrassed. She soothed them, listened to their tales, and laughed with them, sat with them while they ate and allowed them extra sweets. When they were drowsy, for they were very tired from the long walk and the tumultuous day, she dismissed their nurse and herself bathed them, rubbing them rosy with towels and drying their pitch-dark hair. She tucked them into their narrow bed and sat beside them, singing them lullabies from long ago in the Colchian tongue.

The late Greek sun, stealing with its last fingers through the slitted window, touched their high cheekbones, dark gold skin and slanting eyes. Their mother, Daughter of the Sun, sat watching, dreaming wakeful dreams of all that she, in Athenian exile, would never see. And when they were very still, and deep in dreamless sleep, she took up the knife of sacrifice that she had brought from Colchis, and she cut their throats.

When Jason arrived, a distraught and fearful Jason who had run in desperate apprehension from the holocaust of the palace, he found the house still as a tomb and a knot of superstitious, frightened servants gathered outside the doors.

"Is the witch still within the house or has she fled? She will have to hide in the earth below, or fly the air, if she hopes to escape the vengeance coming to her from friends of the murdered king." He received no answer and, in frantic haste, began to batter upon the twice-barred door.

"What seek you?" The voice astonished him, for it was quiet and serene.

"Open the door! I have brought no threat to you. I have come for my children, that I may keep them safe!"

Silence. Then, slowly, the door opened, and Medea stepped forth, dressed in the robes of Hecate's priestess. She was like one carved in stone, who has passed beyond all grief and horror to a kind of peace. In her hand she held the sacrificial knife, and behind her drew a wicker cart, like the funeral carts of Colchis. The bodies of her sons lay upon it, smiling in their endless sleep.

It was at last, for Jason, the moment of truth.

"You . . . hateful . . . *thing*." His voice came slowly in incredulous whisper. "Are you a woman? Have you done this, and can still look upon the sun? Now I see plain, when I took you from a foreign home and brought you to golden Greece, the gods hurled a curse upon me."

"The blame lies with you, Jason, not the gods. The fault is mine, too—I trusted the words of a Greek. But the deeds this day's sun has seen, you brought them on. Long is the answer I might make, did not Zeus the Father already know how much I loved you, and how you repaid that love."

"No Greek woman would have dared such deeds."

"Aye!" Medea's head lifted and her eyes flashed gold. "No Greek would have loved enough to kill, or had the courage. Go, Jason. Go, and live. Life is the curse I put upon you."

He hesitated, and she knew she had won. He did not have the courage—"as I would have," she thought with a flash of contempt—to fall upon her there and kill her. Or to kill himself and face the gods. He was not, in the last analysis, a man of action.

"At least," he said at last, wearily, "give me my sons, that I may bury them and mourn for them."

"They are not yours! You disowned them as half-breeds when you disavowed their mother. They are mine now. And they are safe. Life—and you and I, Jason—can never harm them more."

Before Jason could stop her, she was gone, into the house of death with her dead children. The heavy doors swung shut behind them, and he heard the iron bolts dropped. In moments, smoke began curling through every crack and aperture. Medea had made of the whole house a funeral pyre.

The last Jason saw of her was on the burning roof, an implacable Fury in her bitter triumph, wreathed in smoke like incense from sacrifice. And if the dying sun played tricks upon his eyes, and he saw her through salt brine as she had looked once long before, on a balcony in Colchis, she would never know.

EPILOGUE

AND SO she fled from Corinth. Some there were who swore she flew off from the roof in clouds of fire. Some say she drove a dragon chariot. Some men think she was swept off in the wind by her strange gods.

Be that as it may. The fact remains that she left Corinth, and none did lift a hand to stop her. Perhaps they were ashamed. Perhaps they, and the gods too, thought she had suffered enough already. For she had fallen far in people's eyes, and known great sorrow, and great was the price she'd paid. Perhaps they simply didn't care. People are like that, once the worst is over, and all of us would rather not see the stranger in our midst.

Medea left. She left as she had come, her head held high, unbroken, responsible for her own past, mistress of her own future, which she looked upon with eyes devoid of tears. And if the gods were watching, perhaps they laughed. They hurled no thunderbolts to bar her way.

She went to Athens, to Aegeus. Noble Aegeus, too kind to let the stranger suffer, too kind to ever really understand. In his eyes she still saw mirrored a slender, black-haired girl. The hair grew white with years, but she still walked tall. And she was honored in the city. Some said she brought it blessing. It brought her peace.

Yet sometimes, when the mist blows from the sea, she slips away from her maids and walks the ramparts. Her hair falls free and streams in the wind that whips her veils. She feels salt upon her cheek. And sometimes, suddenly, the mists part, and the sun pierces through the magic blue, and she sees a ship, a strange ship like a great bird flying. With gold on the masts, but none so bright as the hair of the tall young stranger. Bright as a golden fleece. And she dreams of Jason.

Jason. Never was there a man so greatly loved. None so betrayed that love, and none was so repaid. She looks upon him, striding towards her out of the mists of years, and her lips part, and her heart pounds within her, and her blood again is hot and singing in her veins.

For the opposite side of the coin of hate is love. And the stranger we fear is the stranger in our heart, the mirror image of our shadow self.

You ask me how I know these things? I know, for I am old, and some do call me witch. I know them as I lived them, lived and learned too late. You who are young, who take love lightly as a butterfly that can as quickly die, who fling betrayal and hatred before you like skipping stones, who give and take too quickly, too completely, with closed eyes, hear me. I know.

I am Medea.

I am she, and I know, I have known, have been known. These two truths are the children I bequeath you. Hate is the other face of love. The stranger is ourself.

Oh, Jason, most loved, most hated among men, I give you this. And one truth more. Are you laughing, gods? The truth is, such was our love, such the irony of this thing called life, and such my passion, that I would take you now, even now,

were you to come again to me through the mist, and hold out
your hand to me, and speak my name.

Oh, Jason, Jason!

AUTHOR'S
NOTES

T HE STORIES OF the Golden Fleece are myths and, being myths, the truths they contain are larger than human experience and not dependent on logic or facts. They began as primitive man's attempts to "explain the un-explainable"—the nature of man, his relationships to his neigh-bors, the world around him, and divine powers—in terms that he and his world could understand. They began as part of the oral tradition—tales of an earlier, golden time passed down by tutors and grandparents, bards and strolling storytellers for centuries before authors began recording them in written form, and by that time each had acquired innumerable variations as well as certain inviolable conventions. The familiar fairy tale of Cinderella is told today in many ways; the names, the dia-logue and descriptions differ, but always there are the wicked stepparent, the fairy godmother, the midnight curfew, the three nights at the ball and the glass slipper. So it was with Grecian Jason and Colchian Medea, and the Golden Fleece, which bridged their separate worlds.

Strangers Dark and Gold has been based on the three earliest

written accounts of Jason and Medea that have survived intact
to the present day. Apollonius of Rhodes, a citizen of Alexandria, wrote a long epic poem some time in the third century
B.C., called *Argonautica,* or *The Voyage of Argo,* which tells
the events of Chapters 4 through 22. Earlier, in the late fifth
century B.C., the aristocratic Theban poet Pindar wrote his
Fourth Pythian Ode to commemorate the winning of a chariot
race by Arkesilas IV, king of Kyrene and descendant of the
Argonaut Euphamos. Pindar's poem tells of Jason's journey to
Colchis and his winning both Medea and the Fleece, and also
gives many details of his birth and childhood, his arrival in
Iolcus and his first confrontation with Pelias. Also in the fifth
century, Euripides, one of the greatest and perhaps the most
modern of the Greek dramatists, wrote his tragedy *Medea,*
which won third prize in the state dramatic contest in Athens
in 431 B.C. The play, which details the events of the one day
that is described in Chapters 25 through 27, tells also of Medea's
murder of Pelias, the Corinthian exile, and Medea's future life
in Athens.

These three—Apollonius, Pindar, Euripides—were retelling
stories already long familiar to their audiences; each with his
own genius told the tale in his own way, adding details out of
his own insight and imagination, retaining others he knew his
audience expected. They were writing—and this is hard for us
to comprehend—of events that supposedly had taken place in
the dawn of history, in a Greece as far removed from them in
time as their time is from ours today.

I have been faithful to these three accounts as much as possible, filling in gaps wherever possible with the bits and pieces
of references to Jason and Medea found in other early writings.
Where contradictions in accounts occur, I have chosen the ver-
sion that seems most consistent with the whole sweep of Jason
and Medea's story.

There are various versions of the story of Athamas and Ino;
the family relationship between Athamas and Cretheus, and

therefore Jason and Pelias, is told in different ways by modern scholars. Some accounts say that Ino went mad with the Bacchic madness and unknowingly killed her son, Melicertes, by boiling him in a cauldron, thinking him a wild animal that she had caught.

The identities of the Argonauts are part of the great tradition, they are all the greatest heroes of the Greek myths and legends, each bringing to Jason's quest his own special skill. The fact that if all these men had really lived, and all the stories told of them really been true, they could not possibly all have been alive, let alone young, at the same time, is of no matter. Time is immaterial in myths.

According to Euripides, King Aegeus of Athens, when he offers sanctuary to Medea, tells her that he is childless. Aegeus was eventually succeeded on the Athenian throne by his son Theseus, the slayer of the Minotaur and the embodiment of the Athenian masculine ideal. Yet many early writers, though not Apollonius, tell us that Theseus himself was among the Argonauts. Apollonius does have Jason tell Medea the story of Ariadne—the Minoan princess who helps Theseus escape the Labyrinth and eventually is deserted by him.

The geography of *Argo*'s wanderings is fascinating in its accuracies and inaccuracies. The outward journey, as Apollonius describes it, follows sea-routes known to his contemporaries, and can be charted without difficulty on maritime maps. Much of his knowledge of tribes and tribal customs in middle and eastern Europe is accurate; it is possible he was basing his route on the old transcontinental routes used by amber traders, and the descriptions of the Mossynoeci and the routes taken by ancient Egyptian traders he took from Xenophon and Herodotus respectively. Yet Apollonius solves the problem of the Argonauts' crossing the Alps simply by ignoring it; he relied on the conveniently popular belief of the time that all great rivers managed to flow into one another for the convenience of travelers! Apollonius gives almost guidebook descriptions of the various capes, rocks, and rivers passed—until he has *Argo* enter the area of Southern Italy and the Ionian islands, when he becomes amazingly vague, although the territory was well known to travelers of his day. Scholars suggest this is because he was now writing about "Homer's seas"—the geography of the Homeric tales is as inaccurate as the tales themselves are sacred, and a wise writer, even in the third century B.C., was not about to contradict the *Iliad* or *Odyssey*!

Apollonius, who seems more than half in love with his heroine and gives us a sensitive portrayal of a young girl caught in the throes of a first and overpowering love, says that Medea only lured Apsyrtus to his death, but that Jason struck the fatal blow. In Euripides' play, when Medea is throwing up to Jason all she has done for him, she says that she herself murdered her brother for his sake.

Later writers, including Ovid (*Metamorphoses*) and Shakespeare (*The Merchant of Venice*) say that Medea restored a still-living Aeson to his lost youth. Earlier accounts tell the story given here—that Pelias forced Aeson's suicide and Alcimede cursed Pelias and then killed herself. Since Jason never does succeed to the throne of Iolcus, the latter seems most logical. I have attempted to join the two tales by having Medea prepare in advance the potion recorded by Ovid, only to reach Iolcus too late, and had her tell of the potion to the daughters of Pelias in order to induce them to kill their father as Euripides records.

There is, to the best of my knowledge, a complete blank space in the myths between the death of Pelias and the marriage of Jason to Creon's daughter Creusa (also called Glauca). In Euripides' play, a Nurse-narrator and a Chorus of Women tell us the skeletal facts that are given in Chapters 23 and 24.

The sons of Phrixus completely drop from sight after *Argo* returns to Pagasae. Presumably they went to Orchomenos, in compliance with their father's dying wish, and settled there.

The sons of Medea are named either Mermerus and Pheras, or Thessalus and Alcimenes.

Translator E. V. Rieu has pointed out that Apollonius, although remaining faithful to the myths by having the Olympic gods appear and speak to men, apparently knew a great deal about psychology and physiology—always, when such visions come in *Argonautica,* they are after the Argonauts have labored for long hours without food or sleep, or else when, possibly, hallucinatory material had been either swallowed or burned to smoke! He also suggests that Apollonius may have been thinking of the Colossus of Rhodes when he wrote of the man of bronze that Medea destroys and of the Pharos (lighthouse) of Alexandria when he tells of the light that Apollo sends out of the fog to guide *Argo*'s way (both Chapter 22).

In all the versions of the myths, certain things remain: A young man not himself heroic, who dazzles all who look on him and is able to inspire others to do great deeds in his place; the first great Quest—an Impossible Dream fulfilled—that takes all the finest and bravest young men of their time across the world and back, triumphant against unbelievable odds, and set a pattern in Western world literature ever since; a remarkable woman—brilliant, courageous, clever—who sacrifices all for love, only to find that the man she loved was not what she had thought; and culture shock—two opposing cultures, life-styles, values, conflicting with each other and demonstrating that "foreign" and "native," "correct" and "incorrect," "good" and "bad" are relative things, depending on one's point of view.

Above all it is the story of an indomitable and very human being, remarkable in her own and any other time. It is Medea, not Jason, who is the hero. All she does is done not out of selfishness but out of love; all she does that seems witchcraft can be done by skill in homeopathic medicine, psychology, hypnotism and drugs. She, unlike the other tragic heroes, is never brought low by *hubris* (false pride; trying to "be like God"), punished, and then made wise by suffering. Her fate is brought upon her not by the gods but by herself; she knows it and accepts it. Her end and suffering is her own doing, she bears it stoically, she goes on with her head high—not in false pride, but in self-knowledge and self-respect—and she endures.

Even the divine powers, apparently, felt that she had learned her own hard lesson and had suffered enough. As a modern playwright, writing of the old myths, put it, she reached at last the tower beyond tragedy where peace was, and where no more pain could come.

GLOSSARY

Acastus—son of King Pelias and cousin of Jason; an Argonaut.

Acheron—the "river of woe" leading into the underworld; also the name of an area in the underworld.

acropolis—the citadel of any ancient Greek city, usually on high ground and containing all the main sanctuaries.

Aea—the capital city of Colchis.

Aeolus—a famous Greek hero, father of Athamas and grandfather of Phrixus.

Aeson—deposed king of Iolcus and father of Jason.

Aetes—king of Colchis; brother of the enchantress Circe; father of Apsyrtus, Chalciope and Medea. Supposedly the son of Helios the god of the sun.

Aetna, Mt.—a volcanic mountain in Sicily.

Age of Gold—in Greek mythology, the Age of the Titans, ruled by Cronus the father of Zeus, when the world was in eternal spring.

Alcimede—wife of Aeson and mother of Jason.

Alcinous—King of the Phaecians and husband of Queen Arete.

Amazons—a race of woman warriors living in Asia Minor.

Amycus—King of the Bebryces on the Bithynian coast.

Amythaon—son of Cretheus and Tyro, brother of Aeson, uncle of Jason.

Anaurus—river in Thessaly near Larissa, which flows into Gulf of Pagasae.

Aphrodite—goddess of love and beauty, born of the foam of the sea near Cythera and floated on the sea from there to Cyprus. Married to Hephaestus, lame god of the forge; mother of Eros (Cupid).

Apollo—god of prophecy, the arts, healing, light and truth, music, archery. Son of Zeus & Leto, born on the Isle of Delos. Purifier, peacemaker, masculine ideal of beauty, intelligence, strength. Spoke through the oracle of Delphi. Because the god of light, often identified as god of the sun. Drove chariot of the sun across the sky. Also called Phoebus.

Apsyrtus—son and heir of Aetes, king of Colchis. Half-brother of Chalciope and Medea.

Ares—god of war, son of Zeus & Hera. (Roman: Mars)

Arete—queen of Drepane, wife of Alcinous.

Argo—the "blessed ship," built by the Argonaut Argus under supervision of Athene.

Argonauts—name given to the men, all sons of gods and kings, who sailed on *Argo* in search of the Golden Fleece.

Argus—1) a Greek who built the ship *Argo* & sailed on her; 2) eldest son of Phrixus & Chalciope (once the Argonauts reached Colchis, any reference to Argus means the Colchian prince).

Ariadne—princess of Crete who helped Theseus escape from the Labyrinth of the Minotaur and was later deserted by him.

Artemis—goddess of the chase, protector of wild animals, the "divine huntress," also identified with the moon as her brother Apollo was with the sun. Daughter of Zeus & Leto. (Roman: Diana)

Athamas—king of Orchomenus in Boeotia, Greece; father of Phrixus and Helle. Married 1) Nephele, 2) Ino.

Athene—goddess of wisdom, daughter of Zeus (sprang full-grown from his brain at the Tritonian Lagoon in Libya). Patroness of arts and crafts. (Roman: Minerva)

Ausonian Sea—Italian Sea. (Italy = Ausonia)

Boreas—the north wind, father of Zetes & Calais.

Cadmus—founder and king of Thebes in Boeotia, Greece. Married Harmonia, daughter of Ares & Aphrodite; father of Ino, Semele, Agave, Autonoe.

Calypso—a nymph who lived on island of Ogygia.

Cape Canastra—peninsula in northeast Greece between Olympus and Lemnos.

Chalciope—daughter of Aetes, sister of Medea & Apsyrtus, widow of Phrixus, mother of Argus & his brothers; princess of Colchis.

Chaos—the shapeless nothingness that existed before the world was created; ultimately separated into Earth and Heaven. (Gaea & Uranus)

Chiron—a centaur (half man, half horse), son of the Titan Cronos and Philyra; he raised and taught Jason in his cave in Mt. Pelion. Master of hunting, spearmanship, riding, music, prophecy, healing.

Circe—daughter of Helios and Perse, sister of Aetes and aunt of Medea.

A beautiful enchantress who turns men into beasts. (see *Odyssey*)

Colchis—the kingdom of King Aetes, lying at eastern end of the Black Sea, including part of the Caucasus Mts.

Corcyra—modern Corfu, also called Drepane or Macris.

Corcyra (Black)—island off coast of Yugoslavia, northwest of Corcyra.

Creon—king of Corinth and father of Creusa.

Creusa—daughter of Creon, king of Corinth, second wife of Jason. Also called Glauca.

Cycanian Rocks—the Clashing Rocks, the legendary Symplegades, at northern end of Bosporus.

Delphi—shrine near Mt. Parnassus, called "earth's navel stone," thought by Greeks to be center of the earth. Most sacred and most famous shrine to Apollo and site of his oracle.

Delphic oracle—priestess who presided over shrine at Delphi. Apollo's messages were thought to be transmitted to her while she was in a trance caused by vapor rising from cleft in rocks, possibly augmented by smoke from burning drugs; her unintelligible syllables were translated by a listening priest.

Dionysus—god of wine and the fruits of the vine, and of ecstasy. Son of Zeus and Semele, the daughter of Cadmus. Associated with the two results of wine—freedom and ecstatic joy; savage brutality. A fertility god identified with a death-and-resurrection cult and with the emotional frenzy of the Maenads. Also god of the theater; the first tragedies were performed in his honor.

Elysium—the Elysian Fields, the "good place" or "blessed place," home of the good and heroic in the Underworld.

Endymion—a beautiful youth beloved of the moon, who caused him to fall into an endless sleep so she might visit him whenever she wished without his knowing.

Eridanus—probably the river Po in northern Italy.

Fates—the three immortal sisters who wove the pattern of men's lives. Clotho, the spinner, spun the thread of life. Lachesis, the dispenser of lots, chose each human's destiny. Atropos, the unturnable, carried the shears and cut the thread to terminate life.

Furies—the Erinyes, born of the blood of Uranus when he was slain by his son, the Titan Cronus. They lived in the Underworld, where they punished evildoers, and also pursued sinners upon earth—especially those who transgressed against the unwritten laws of instinct and blood loyalty (killing a blood relative, violating sanctuary, killing a guest, etc.). Traditionally considered inexorable but just—possibly personifications of conscience. Usually portrayed as three women: Tisiphone, Megaera, Alecto.

Hades—1) king of the underworld and husband of Persephone. 2) The underworld itself, the kingdom of the dead, which lay beneath the secret places of the earth. Divided into three regions: Tartaros, the place of torment; Erebus or Acheron, the vale of shadows; Elysium, the place of blessedness.

Harpies—the "hounds of Zeus," winged creatures with hooked claws and beaks and a loathsome stench, who persecute Phineus by stealing and defiling his food.

Hecate—underworld goddess, patroness of witchcraft, Goddess of the Dark of the Moon, Goddess of the Crossroads, possibly one of the Titans. A fertility goddess associated with Demeter (Ceres).

Hecatonchires—the hundred-handed monsters with fifty heads, sons of Gaea and Uranus who imprisoned them in a secret place beneath the earth.

Helios—the sun god, father of Aetes, Circe, Pasiphae, Phaethon, Augeias. Sometimes confused in legend with Apollo.

Hellas—old name for Greece.

Helle—daughter of Athamas and Nephele, sister of Phrixus who fell from the back of the Golden Ram and was drowned in the strait separating Europe and Asia that was later named Hellespont in her honor.

Hephaestus—the lame blacksmith god, son of Zeus and Hera, husband of Aphrodite, who made the armor of the Olympic gods. His home and forge have been identified with various volcanoes. A kindly, ugly, peace-loving god, patron of craftsmen.

Hera—sister-wife of Zeus, queen of the gods. Protector of marriage and married women; known for her jealousy and long-held grudges.

Hercynian—German.

Hermes—the messenger god, son of Zeus and Maia. Known for speed, cleverness, cunning; a master trickster; god of the marketplace and tradesmen; god of dreams.

Hesperides—daughters of the Titan Atlas who guarded the sacred golden apple trees; Hespere, Erythus & Aegle.

Hyperion—one of the Titans, father of the sun.

Hypsipyle—princess of Lemnos, daughter of Thoas, in love with Jason.

Illyria—northeast shore of Adriatic Sea, now part of Yugoslavia.

Ino—daughter of Cadmus, married Athamas king of Orchomenus. Stepmother of Phrixus & Helle, mother of Learchus and Melicertes.

Iolcus—city near north shore of Gulf of Pagasae, capital of kingdom ruled by Aeson and then Pelias. Archeological excavations have revealed the city existed from the time of the Bronze Age. (c. 2500 B.C.)

Iris—the messenger of the gods; the rainbow.

Italian Sea—probably the Adriatic.

Jason—son of Alcimede and Aeson; raised in exile by Chiron; returned to Iolcus to claim throne from Pelias; traveled on *Argo* to Colchis where he married Medea & obtained the Golden Fleece; returned to

Iolcus; went into exile in Corinth where he put aside Medea and married Creusa.

Lemnos—a large island in the northern Aegean Sea.

Medea—a sorceress, priestess of Hecate and princess of Colchis. Daughter of Aetes; younger sister of Apsyrtus and Chalciope. She fell in love with Jason; helped him obtain Golden Fleece; eloped with him; murdered Apsyrtus to aid their escape; was married to Jason on Corcyra; returned with him to Iolcus where she caused the murder of Pelias; killed her sons and Creusa to avenge herself on Jason's remarriage.

Medusa—one of the three Gorgons, winged women with snakes for hair, whose dread appearance turned all who looked at them to stone.

Minoan—Cretan.

Minyae—"descendants to Minyas"; name given to the Argonauts.

Morpheus—son and messenger of the god of sleep.

Nephele—first wife of Athamas, mother of Phrixus and Helle.

Ocean—a river that was supposed to encircle the earth; also the Titan who was lord of the River Ocean.

Olympus—highest mountain in Greece, located in Thessaly, believed to be the home of the Olympic gods.

Orchomenus—son of Minyas and king of the city in Boeotia named in his honor.

Orion—a huntsman of Artemis who after his death was placed in the sky as a constellation.

Pagasae—harbor of Iolcus where *Argo* was built and launched.

Pelias—son of Tyro, supposedly fathered by Poseidon; half-brother of Aeson; uncle of Jason.

Mt. Pelion—mountain in Thessaly, home of Chiron.

Pheras—son of Cretheus & Tyro, brother of Aeson, uncle of Jason.

Phineus—blind prophet visited by Argonauts on coast of Thynia.

Phoebus—"the brilliant, shining one," a title given to Apollo.

Phrixus—son of Athamas and Nephele and brother of Helle, given over for sacrifice by his father as result of stepmother Ino's trick, but saved with his sister by the Golden Ram sent by Hermes. In Colchis he sacrificed the Ram to Zeus, gave the fleece to Aetes, and married Aetes' daughter Chalciope. They had four sons: Argus, Cytissorus, Melas, Phrontis. On his deathbed he told his sons to travel to Orchomenus and claim the estate of their dead grandfather Athamas.

Poseidon—Olympic god, son of Cronus and Rhea; brother of Zeus; husband of Amphitrite; chief god of the sea and god of horses. (Roman: Neptune)

Prometheus—son of the Titan Iapetus; stole fire from the gods to give to man and was punished by Zeus by being chained to a mountain peak in the Caucasus where every day an eagle tore out his liver, which grew back by night. His name means "foresight"; he represents man's free-spirited defiance of the gods despite all costs.

Propontis—the sea of Marmora.

Rhea—a Titan, sister-wife of Cronus; replaced her mother, Gaea, as an earth-mother goddess of fertility; especially associated with her daughter Demeter (Ceres), the goddess of corn (wheat) and the harvest. Mt. Dindymum on the Isle of the Doliones was one of her seats of worship.

Scylla—a nymph, changed by jealous Circe into a fearsome monster rooted to rock, with serpents' and dogs' heads growing from her body, designed to destroy all ships and sailors passing near; a rock on the southwestern tip of Italy near the northeast tip of Sicily.

Sirens—beautiful women with spellbinding voices who lived on an island in the sea and lured sailors to their deaths on the rocks.

Sporades—scattered island group in the Aegean Sea north of Crete, including Thera (Santorin) and Anaphe.

Stoechades—the Isles d'Hyeres off the Mediterranean coast, east of Toulon.

Stymphalian Birds—birds sacred to Mars with brazen claws and beaks, who used feathers as arrows and ate human flesh. They were driven off by Hercules as his fifth labor, and eluded by the Argonauts by a trick.

Syrtis (Gulf)—probably the Gulf of Sydra on coast of Tripoli.

Thebes—1) The city founded by Cadmus in Boeotia, north of Athens; 2) a smaller city (*not* Cadmus'), near Pagasae and Iolcus in Thessaly; 3) the ancient capital of Egypt.

Thermodon (R)—the modern river Termeh, flowing into Black Sea east of River Iris.

Thessaly—a large territory in northern Greece, south of Macedonia and north of Aetolia and Locris.

Titans—the twelve Elder Gods, children of Gaea and Uranus and ancestors of the Olympic gods; of great size and strength—like men, only grander.

Triton—a sea god, son of Poseidon and Amplitrite.

Tritonial Lagoon—a large salt lake on coast of Libya.

Tyrrhenian Sea—the Italian Sea, off west coast of Italy. Tyrrhenia was the Greek name for Etruria (Tuscany).

Unfriendly Sea—the Black Sea.

Uranus—the overhanging heavens, husband of Gaea.

Zeus—Olympian god, son of Cronus & Rhea; husband of Hera. The supreme ruler, Lord of the Sky, the Rain-God, the Cloud-Gatherer; fount of kingly power, patron of rulers, establisher of laws, order, justice.